PRAIS
BIG TROUBL

"Because Allen Jackson is one of the most insightful and dynamic pastors on the planet, when he speaks, I try to listen. I'm never disappointed. And you won't be disappointed by his latest book, *Big Trouble Ahead*, as he boldly describes the hostility towards biblical Christianity we face today. But true to his always Christ-centered message, Pastor Jackson reminds us that the 'big trouble ahead' should not rob believers of their hope and expectation. Pastor Allen Jackson is the real deal—a man of rare gifts with even rarer humility."

—MIKE HUCKABEE, FORMER GOVERNOR OF ARKANSAS, 2008 PRESIDENTIAL CANDIDATE, *NEW YORK TIMES* BESTSELLING AUTHOR, AND HOST OF POPULAR WEEKLY TALK SHOW *HUCKABEE*

"Pastor Allen Jackson is an uncompromising voice for truth in a generation where those in authority haven't 'played it straight.' In *Big Trouble Ahead* Jackson lays out current events through the lens of the Bible and offers a guide to help you wisely chart new territory."

—ERIC METAXAS, #1 *NEW YORK TIMES* BESTSELLING AUTHOR AND HOST OF THE NATIONALLY SYNDICATED *ERIC METAXAS RADIO SHOW*

"In a world that seems to have completely lost its mind, Pastor Allen Jackson points us back to the steadfast hope we have in Christ. Not in Congress. Not in cancel culture. Not in conflict or controversy. In Christ."

—DAVE RAMSEY, BESTSELLING AUTHOR AND RADIO HOST

"Allen Jackson understands the times without being intimidated by them. He's honest, uncompromising, unafraid, yet optimistic. I've always thought of Allen as remarkably tough yet surprisingly tender. In reading this book I've discovered some of his secrets. He understands what's happening in the world, but his heart and mind are anchored in the Word, which cannot be shaken. After reading this book, I'm with him! There is big truth inside *Big Trouble Ahead*! And it can make a big difference in your life."

—ROB MORGAN, AUTHOR AND PASTOR

"There is no greater modern-day political prophet than my friend Allen Jackson. He has his finger on the pulse of the culture. America should pay heed to his message in *Big Trouble Ahead*."

—TODD STARNES, BESTSELLING AUTHOR AND RADIO HOST

"My dear friend Pastor Allen Jackson has recognized the ideological and spiritual basis of the conflagration we face in America. In his latest literary work, *Big Trouble Ahead*, Pastor Jackson lucidly identifies the issues facing America and how God's people can be the solution. Pastor Jackson reminds us of the men of the cloth who served in the Black Robe Regiment during our Revolutionary War. Like Pastor Jackson, I see great opportunities for the body of Christ to be the salt and light for America, enabling a restoration and redemption of the longest running constitutional republic the world has ever known. Now is the time for Christians to be strong and of good courage. My brother Allen Jackson is reminding us of God's admonition in Isaiah 54:17, 'No weapon formed against us shall prosper.' I encourage all true Americans and Christians to read *Big Trouble Ahead* and find your resolve to persevere!"

—LIEUTENANT COLONEL ALLEN B. WEST (US ARMY RETIRED), MEMBER OF THE 112TH US CONGRESS, AND FORMER CHAIRMAN OF THE REPUBLICAN PARTY OF TEXAS

"This book is sure to wake up the church from its comfortable nap. Allen Jackson makes sense of the disorientation we're experiencing from the unprecedented volume, velocity, and vitriol of problems in front of us. God now has our attention—how will we respond? *Big Trouble Ahead* provides a healthy assessment of our current reality and a confident, faithful way forward for those who will courageously stand with Christ."

—JASON YATES, CEO OF MY FAITH VOTES

BIG
TROUBLE
AHEAD

A REAL PLAN *for* FLOURISHING
IN A TIME OF FEAR AND DECEPTION

ALLEN JACKSON

NELSON
BOOKS
An Imprint of Thomas Nelson

Published in Nashville, Tennessee, by Nelson Books, an imprint of Thomas Nelson. Nelson Books and Thomas Nelson are registered trademarks of HarperCollins Christian Publishing, Inc.

Published in association with Yates & Yates, www.yates2.com.

Thomas Nelson titles may be purchased in bulk for educational, business, fundraising, or sales promotional use. For information, please email SpecialMarkets@ThomasNelson.com.

Library of Congress Cataloging-in-Publication Data

Names: Jackson, Allen, 1958- author.
Title: Big trouble ahead : a real plan for flourishing in a time of fear and deception / Allen Jackson.
Description: Nashville, Tennessee : Thomas Nelson, [2022] | Summary: "The church in America is being shaken like never before, from rampant deception and lawlessness to intense cultural pressures to conform and compromise. Pastor Allen Jackson reveals a biblical perspective on the events unfolding in our nation, and shows readers how they can hold onto hope and flourish, even in the midst of the shaking"-- Provided by publisher.
Identifiers: LCCN 2022007561 (print) | LCCN 2022007562 (ebook) | ISBN 9781400217281 (pb) | ISBN 9781400217298 (epub) | ISBN 9781400217304 (Audiobook)
Subjects: LCSH: United States--Church history--21st century. | Christianity and culture--United States--History--21st century.
Classification: LCC BR526 .J323 2022 (print) | LCC BR526 (ebook) | DDC 277.308/3--dc23/eng/20220325
LC record available at https://lccn.loc.gov/2022007561
LC ebook record available at https://lccn.loc.gov/2022007562

Printed in the United States of America

24 25 26 27 28 LBC 8 7 6 5 4

This book is dedicated to the overcomers, the remarkable people of God throughout the earth who choose to persevere in the face of adversity. They model for all Christ-followers the determined faith that is necessary to triumph in the midst of turmoil and confusion. Our redemption is drawing nearer, let us lift up our eyes in anticipation.

CONTENTS

INTRODUCTION

I have never experienced an Easter Sunday like the one I experienced in 2020. And frankly, I pray that we will never need to repeat the experiences of that day.

Easter is the pivotal event in the Christian story, and it should be celebrated with more enthusiasm than the Super Bowl. In a normal year our Easter celebration is a culmination of months of planning: Making sure there will be friendly faces at the doors as well as trained volunteers in the children's areas. Sorting out the logistics of traffic and parking. You get the picture: hours and hours of planning in order for the staff and hundreds of volunteers to provide a wonderful experience for everyone who comes to our campus.

But that Easter Sunday morning was different.

We had scuttled our plans for multiple services spread across the weekend to accommodate the crowds. The parking lots were virtually empty. The coffee shop, usually abuzz with people, sat silent. The rooms where our children and youth normally gather were uncharacteristically dark and quiet. I walked through the building and was reminded again that the life of any church is not the building, but the people who fill it—and they were not there.

The small group of people that is necessary to pull off a livestream broadcast gathered in the otherwise empty main sanctuary. We prayed that we would present an Easter worship experience that would be uplifting and encouraging in such an unusual circumstance. We desperately needed that for ourselves too.

The worship team did a fantastic job that morning. As their last notes faded away and they left the platform, I walked out and took my usual place. But instead of facing a room full of joyful faces, I looked out across an empty space. On this day I would be speaking to a red light staring at me from the back of the room.

It is always a joy and a privilege to share the story of Jesus' resurrection and tell of the hope it offers. It is good to remind ourselves that life triumphs over death and faith is more powerful than fear. But Easter presents a challenge for a pastor, too, because the story never changes, and everyone is familiar with it.

This year offered a different challenge: we had been told that millions of Americans might die during the pandemic that showed no signs of slowing down. I knew that this year I wouldn't need to be clever. This year I would need to offer hope to the unseen people who were watching from their homes—people who were anxious, confused, and hurting in ways I would never know. This year the simple truth of the power of the resurrection would be more essential than ever.

But that day also reinforced in all of us that we could be facing a "new normal," at least for the foreseeable future. It was a wake-up call for me. I had wrongly imagined that our ability to gather where we wanted and when we wanted was an enduring freedom in our nation, guaranteed by our Constitution's First

Amendment. I thought that could never be interrupted—until it was.

I have repented for my spirit of presumption and my arrogance. Now when I have the privilege of being with God's people, I understand the tremendous honor it is. I will never take it for granted again. As for World Outreach Church, we will meet inside or outside, in a parking lot or on a field, early or late. Wherever, whenever—we will meet.

Over time I have had the opportunity to reflect on what had brought us to that point. How had churches, including ours, seemingly become optional, just another extracurricular activity that could be shut down at will? Why did some churches stand firm in the face of opposition and insist on their right to meet, while others did not? Why did some churches go to extreme measures in order to meet in safe ways, while others said, "We'll see you when it's over"?

The challenge was not just in the attitude of church leaders; it was evident throughout the community of faith. We accepted a message of self-preservation and forfeited an opportunity to serve. COVID-19 was not just a "snow day" allowing a bit of personal time and the illusion of "I'll work from home." COVID was presented as a threat to our well-being—and Christians have a hope beyond time, which equips us to respond to such threats with courage. If two million Americans had been lost to COVID in the initial wave of the pandemic, as some predicted was possible, the church would have had a responsibility to respond as servants prepared to meet needs—not huddle in place.

Freedom and liberty are not bestowed by governments; they come from almighty God. Therefore, in times of turmoil, the responses of God's people are essential if liberties and freedom are to be preserved. I believe COVID-19 was a tremor, a fore-shock of the challenges ahead. I pray we are learning lessons that will enable us to respond with faith, boldness, and courage.

God has blessed America during this pandemic. While the suffering has been immense and tragic, the direst predictions have been averted. But no one with open eyes and listening ears can deny that we still are living through a season of shaking. You don't have to be particularly prophetic or discerning to see that there is trouble all around us. A global pandemic, widespread deception, blatant immorality, unchecked lawlessness, an unstable economy, trampled civil rights, indoctrination of children—all of those define our current reality. And the Bible says there is more trouble ahead.

WHY ARE WE SURPRISED?

We shouldn't be surprised by the trouble we are experiencing. Seasons of trouble span the entirety of human history. And many Christians around the world have experienced harassment and persecution that the American church is only beginning to feel. The Bible tells us that every generation will experience trouble; the more formal religious word is *tribulation*.

We're told that the final tribulation before Jesus' return at the end of the age will be like nothing humanity has ever experienced. Jesus said, "For nation will rise against nation, and kingdom against kingdom, and there will be famines and earthquakes in various places. But all these things are merely the beginning of birth pains. . . . For then there will be a great tribulation, such as has not occurred since the beginning of the world until now, nor ever will again" (Matthew 24:7–8, 21 NASB).

Another way of understanding the word *tribulation* is "big trouble." Jesus cautioned us, warning that His followers would face "big trouble" immediately prior to His return. Jesus was always honest with people about what they could expect if they followed Him. He told them they should count on being persecuted, just as the prophets had been persecuted generations before, but that they would be rewarded for their perseverance: "Blessed are you when people insult you and persecute you, and falsely say all kinds of evil against you because of Me. Rejoice and be glad, for your reward in heaven is great; for in this same way they persecuted the prophets who were before you" (Matthew 5:11–12 NASB).

Jesus' own life was marked by conflict and mistreatment and harassment, but He understood His purpose and persevered, even until death. He told His disciples, "These things I have spoken to you so that in Me you may have peace. In the world you have tribulation, but take courage; I have overcome the world" (John 16:33 NASB).

Later, after the apostle Paul had been stoned and left for dead, he recovered and began his preaching ministry again, "strengthening the souls of the disciples, encouraging them to continue in the faith, and saying, 'It is through many tribulations that we must enter the kingdom of God'" (Acts 14:22 NASB).

And John, before he described the vision Jesus gave him of the end of the age, reminded us of what he had experienced and why he was living in exile: "I, John, your brother and fellow participant in the tribulation and kingdom and perseverance in Jesus, was on the island called Patmos because of the word of

God and the testimony of Jesus" (Revelation 1:9 NASB). John, our "brother and fellow participant in the tribulation," said that persevering through trouble will be necessary for all who belong to God's kingdom.

I believe that we are approaching the end of the age. But I'm not interested in trying to convince you of that, or in engaging in a discussion of whether we will be here to experience the final tribulation the Bible describes. Because no matter the timing and sequence of the last days, these are *our* last days. We are given just one brief lifetime to serve God and advance His kingdom purposes. If we are so privileged to be the generation that is called to stand on behalf of our Lord prior to His return, I pray that we will do so with joy.

LOOKING FORWARD

People who are outside the kingdom of God are without hope and have much to fear about the end of the age. But we, as followers of Jesus, are not without hope!

While we know we can expect to suffer for the name of Jesus, we are strengthened by the Holy Spirit. We can face whatever comes with hopeful expectation because we know how the story ends: "But when these things begin to take place, straighten up and lift up your heads, because your redemption is drawing near" (Luke 21:28 NASB).

It is absolutely necessary that we remain watchful and alert, because no one knows the day of Jesus' coming, and He will not come when we expect Him to (Matthew 24:42–44). Instead of causing us to look toward the sky for signs and wonders, this should provide us with daily motivation to persevere in honoring God with our lives. Paul, who had firsthand experience of persecution for the sake of Jesus, reminded us: "Be joyful in hope, patient in affliction, faithful in prayer" (Romans 12:12).

Finally, remember that when we face trials for the name of Jesus and persevere, we will be blessed and rewarded: "Blessed is a man who perseveres under trial; for once he has been approved, he will receive the crown of life which the Lord has promised to those who love Him" (James 1:12 NASB).

The bottom line is that there is big trouble ahead. I can't help but think of what would be said of our generation if the pages of our Bible extended to tell our story. Would our generation stand and be counted on the side of the kingdom? Would we be prepared for action? Would we be overcomers or overlookers? That's yet to be answered.

Let's explore what's beneath the shaking in our world and how we can walk into the future with confidence.

CHAPTER 1

OUR TRUST ERODED

At that time many will turn away from the faith and will betray and hate each other, and many false prophets will appear and deceive many people.

—MATTHEW 24:10-11

I t's one of the most famous movie scenes of all time.

Dorothy and Toto, the Tin Man, the Scarecrow, and the Cowardly Lion are in the throne room of the Wizard of Oz. They have done as the Wizard asked and proved themselves worthy by bringing him the broomstick of the Wicked Witch of the West. Now they expect him to keep his promises to them for a way home, a heart, a brain, and courage.

"Not so fast! Not so fast!" the Wizard says. "I'll have to give the matter a little thought. Go away and come back tomorrow!"

"Tomorrow? Oh, but I want to go home now," Dorothy

replies to the Wizard, whose frightful face is projected high in front of them.

"You've had plenty of time already!" the Tin Man adds.

"Do not arouse the wrath of the Great and Powerful Oz!" the Wizard shouts as flames shoot out from around the throne, lightning flashes, and thunder roars. "I said come back tomorrow!"

"If you were really great and powerful, you'd keep your promises!" Dorothy says.

"Do you presume to criticize the Great Oz? You ungrateful creatures! Think yourselves lucky that I'm giving you an audience tomorrow instead of twenty years from now!"

Curious little Toto begins to pull back a curtain, and we see the Wizard. He is yelling into a microphone and furiously manipulating levers and switches in order to create the sound and fury meant to overwhelm and intimidate his audience into submission.[1]

You know the rest of the story. The Wizard is forced to admit that he is just a man from Kansas who arrived in Oz by accident when his hot air balloon was blown off course. He created a beautiful kingdom for himself—one where he could rule without question—and has controlled its citizens from behind the curtain ever since.

The Wizard was a true master of deception, and he might never have been exposed if Toto had not pulled back the curtain.

WIDESPREAD DECEPTION

Americans are walking through a period of deception that is unprecedented in my lifetime. It is fueled by evil, and it is far more serious than a movie character behind a curtain. Not that long ago we were surprised and shocked by blatant displays of deception; now deception is operating boldly and openly. The demand for unthinking, unquestioning obedience. The desire to silence opposing voices and crush dissent. In ways we've never seen before, our freedoms to gather, to speak, and to learn are being threatened.

Deceptive statements disguised as fact flood over us on a daily basis, and they're coming from every direction. Sometimes they are outright lies fabricated with the intent to deceive or cover up. Sometimes they are assertions based in fact, but they have been manipulated by masterful spin doctors to support a certain agenda. We're told by voices of authority to "Come back tomorrow!" only to receive information that contradicts what we heard today. And sometimes deception is nothing more than a belief or opinion we assume is fact because it came from a famous person's Twitter feed.

I often meet Christians who are naive enough to think it is not possible for them to be deceived. "I've been around too long and seen too much," they say. Or, "I'm too smart to fall for that. I can tell the difference between what is real and what is not." Or even, "That person wouldn't lie!"

If you're one of those people, and you believe you're beyond

If you're not aware, if you're not watching, if you're not listening, if you're not thinking—the tidal wave of deception will sweep you away and pull you under.

being fooled because of your age, your clever intellect, or your level of sophistication about the things of the world, you have already shown that you are subject to deception. I understand the temptation to close your eyes, put your hands over your ears, and choose not to think about it. But if you're not willing to pull back the curtain—if you're not aware, if you're not watching, if you're not listening, if you're not thinking—the tidal wave of deception will sweep you away and pull you under.

Here are a few examples of the sea of misleading information that is swirling around us.

A Global Pandemic . . . A Changing Landscape

The coronavirus outbreak that has dominated our world since early 2020 is very real. No one of sound mind can argue with that. SARS-CoV-2 first appeared in Wuhan, China, in 2019, and was dubbed COVID-19. It has caused millions of deaths worldwide, and hundreds of millions of people have been sickened.

But the jumble of confusing information we're given about COVID-19 changes day to day, week to week, and month to month. It has become politicized and varies from city to city, state to state, and nation to nation. In America, one government organization says this, and another one says that, while they all claim to be "following the science" and speaking with authority. The Centers for Disease Control and Prevention (CDC) pledges to "base all public health decisions on the highest quality scientific data that is derived openly and objectively," but its messages are riddled with inconsistency.[2]

These tactics appear intentional in order to overwhelm, daze, and confuse. They remind me of a military tactic made famous by Germany during World War II. Blitzkrieg, or "lightning war,"

4

is a strategy of warfare that intends to marshal all your forces against one objective, then strike ferociously in order to over-whelm, overpower, and crush your enemy as quickly as possible. I cannot help but see some parallels between that and the information coming from our government.

We are the victims of censorship in ways we have never seen. Without apology or embarrassment, government agencies and spokespersons at every level have intentionally hidden and manipulated the truth in order to keep us from knowing what is real, what is dangerous, and what is not. The deceptions have filtered down and played out in virtually every aspect of our lives.

The confusion regarding masks and vaccines would be funny if it were not so serious. The stress health-care workers in COVID units feel as facilities are overwhelmed is unimaginable to anyone who hasn't experienced it. Families have said their final goodbyes over cell phones. Serious conditions including mental health problems, heart disease, cancer, and substance abuse have gone undiagnosed and untreated because people were afraid or not allowed to enter a medical facility.

Turning homes into both schoolrooms and workplaces has been stressful for parents and children. The learning loss many students have experienced will have long-term effects. The Great Resignation has seen waves of workers leave their jobs for a variety of reasons.[3] Companies have redesigned office space in order to abide by government recommendations for workers who may not come back.

Churches have struggled to minister in their communities and meet the needs of their members while following changing guidelines. Many people lived in isolation for over a year, including the vulnerable elderly. Weddings and funerals were postponed. Holidays have been celebrated over conference calls. Families have become alienated and estranged over differing views.

Businesses have closed, some never to reopen. Workers have been laid off or let go. Vehicles have been repossessed. Mortgages have been foreclosed. Renters have been evicted. Landlords have gone bankrupt.

Supply chains have been dramatically reconfigured, causing disruptive changes in everything from manufacturing to distribution. Travel and restaurant restrictions have created uncertainty and cost many people in the hospitality industry their jobs.

We will never know the full extent of mental health crises, suicides, family breakups, hunger, homelessness, crime, bankruptcy, and other tragedies that have been brought on by the tangled web of a global pandemic that came to every town and reached into every home and family.

Politics—or Political Warfare?

The campaigns that precede elections have come to define deception, with millions of dollars as the price tag. Party A wants you to believe something is true, and they will use any means to convince you they are right. Party B wants you to believe the opposite is true, and they will use any means to discredit Group A and convince you *they* are right. Party C says you can't trust either of them. All of them claim they want what is best for you!

However, when elected, many politicians and the government agencies acting under their authority don't put our national interests first; their primary goals are personal gain, consolidating their influence, and keeping their party in power. With their jobs and futures on the line, it seems to be difficult for many people operating in the political realm to uphold the truth and act with integrity.

Climate Change—or Control of the Free Market?

Weather reporting has become so much more than "Cloudy with a chance of rain tomorrow. Better take an umbrella!" The science around climate change dominates our weather forecasting institutions. It has become politicized and used as a tool for deceiving and frightening the public. "Kids are terrified, anxious, and depressed about climate change. Whose fault is that?" Jason Plautz asked in the *Washington Post*.[4]

There is no doubt that the world's climate is changing, but that is nothing new; the world's climate has been changing since the beginning of time. Climate study with the aim of controlling that change has been elevated until it has become a virtual religion. That worldview teaches that everything should be subordinated and subjected to climate control measures. The irony is that while we can predict general weather patterns, we cannot predict with specificity tomorrow's rainfall or where a tornado will touch down—yet we imagine that with great precision we can predict climate outcomes a decade or more away. The travesty is that political and industrial forces across the political spectrum use the arrogance of a few and the fear of many to manipulate various situations for their own selfish goals.

Education—or Indoctrination?

Education shapes our future, and anyone seeking an education for themselves or their children, even in a publicly funded school, must claw their way through a morass of political correctness.

7

Examples abound of conservative viewpoints of faculty and students being condemned or silenced while left-leaning opinions are given much wider latitude. Christian parents did not push back when Christmas parties were replaced by holiday or winter parties, and now their children are being taught yoga and meditation. Many teachers are not allowed to address their classroom as "boys and girls" for fear of offending students who are confused about their gender. And the proponents of teaching Critical Race Theory, which categorizes "individuals into groups of oppressors and victims," seek to make race the "prism" through which students are taught to "analyze all aspects of American life."[5]

Respect for Authority—or Lawlessness?

Law enforcement is under fire. The very people who put their lives on the line every day to protect us are no longer welcome in many places in America. Yes, there are bad apples in law enforcement, as in every field. But activists insist that in addition to punishing the individuals who do wrong, police departments should be defunded. As officers work in atmospheres of hatred and disrespect, crime rates in some locales are soaring.[6] After Portland, Oregon, dissolved a police unit designed to focus on gun violence, the number of shootings rose to two and a half times higher than the year before.[7]

Reporting News—or Reciting Propaganda?

The media was once a trusted part of our society. We expected news organizations to report from a reasonably neutral perspective, or at least report more than one side of a story. Today, news outlets are owned by large corporations that have overarching agendas. Those outlets are in the business of producing stories that support the corporate agenda, and it's very disorienting unless you recognize what those agendas are.

During March Madness 2021, *USA Today* published an opinion piece from their Sports Media Group's Race and Inclusion editor. She suggested that people should protest against the Oral Roberts University men's basketball team, one of the "Cinderella stories" of the tournament, because of the school's "archaic standards of behavior" that are "wildly out of line with modern society." She was offended by the Christian school's "prejudiced teachings and moral regressiveness" that make it a "relic of the past."[8]

The desire among up-and-coming journalists to simply present a fair and accurate news report is decreasing, while other motives are on the rise. A study of students' motivations for pursuing a career in journalism showed that the first reason was "self-fulfillment and maximizing their own talents." The second was wanting "to improve the world and have a job that others respect and admire." Third were the students who wanted to be famous. Fourth, and last, were the students who were more interested in creating a quality news product than any gratification they might get from it.[9]

Social Media—or Social Manipulation?

Social media platforms have been growing steadily in popularity since they were introduced. The global pandemic only accelerated their growth as people looked for ways to stay connected to family, friends, and the outside world. Over 3.6 billion people around the world use social media, and that number is projected to reach 4.41 billion in 2025. Facebook still claims the highest number of users, at 2.74 billion, and those users are targeted by nine million active advertisers.[10]

It can be very difficult to determine what is real and what

is not on social media, and what simply "went viral" because of its popular appeal, or outrageousness, or entertainment value. People tend to align themselves with sites and personalities who support the views they already hold, and the platforms themselves censor and promote certain content. It is challenging to find the truth in that kind of environment. I am grateful for the way our church has been able to expand our reach through social media, but I also am careful to consider what I see there.

Unfortunately, deception is not limited to the secular arena. Churches, in a widespread way, are rejecting holiness and orthodoxy in favor of tolerance and inclusion. "Progressive" denominations that were once biblically orthodox no longer accept the divinity of Jesus, His uniqueness as the incarnate Son of God, and His redemptive work on the cross. His crucifixion and physical death happened, they agree, but His resurrection? Maybe. Or it might just be a good story.

"There is more than one path to spiritual enlightenment," many say. "Give us a try and see if we're a good fit. Or look elsewhere for something you like better. It's all good—unless it's one of those crazy churches where they actually believe in the authority of the Bible!" Many of those same groups reject the biblical view of human sexuality. The sign in front may say "church," but if we do not affirm and teach the truth of God's Word, we add to the confusion and fail in our assignment.

FEELING DIZZY YET?

This widespread deception leaves us feeling completely disoriented. The places we thought we could turn to for truth have left us wondering if they are truth-tellers after all. We're not sure who to believe, or what to think, or where to look for truth. It's very unsettling, and it leaves us feeling weary—physically, mentally, emotionally, and spiritually.

A common response is, "Let's not argue about what's true and false, right and wrong. Let's just try to hang on until we get past this. Maybe when we get through this rough patch, we'll be in a more stable place. Maybe we'll have a clearer picture. Maybe the truth will be more obvious then. Or maybe all the sides will come together and find a middle ground."

But the message of the Bible is that you can't negotiate with evil—and that is what deception is. The only thing that evil will yield to is a power greater than itself. So the solution—the only answer to deception—is truth. And God is the only source of ultimate truth.

> **The only thing that evil will yield to is a power greater than itself.**

THERE IS GOOD NEWS!

You may feel like you have been battered and bruised by the season we are experiencing. That is because you have! But God's Word offers us assurance and hope. The apostle Paul, who was no stranger to adversity, wrote, "Who shall separate us from the love of Christ? Shall trouble or hardship or persecution or famine or nakedness or danger or sword? . . . No, in all these things we are more than conquerors through him who loved us" (Romans 8:35, 37).

More than conquerors—I like that! It may feel as if the world is an unstable and frightening place right now, but I see two very hopeful signs. First, God is shaking everything around us and exposing all the things that are unstable and temporary and not of His kingdom. It is uncomfortable in the moment, but it will help us see things from His perspective and align ourselves more closely with Him. Second, He is at work around the world and revealing Himself in ways that are extraordinary in the unfolding history of the church. We will discuss these reasons for optimism later, but for now, hang on to that hope!

SOME VITAL QUESTIONS

I assure you that we can do more than just survive this season; we can triumph. I believe that when you finish this book, you will have a renewed enthusiasm for your relationship with the Lord. I believe that your faith in Him will be greater than it ever has been. I believe that you will have a fresh sense of His plans and purposes for your life. In order to accomplish that, I encourage you to ask yourself these questions:

1. Am I awake and aware of what He is doing around me?
2. Are my eyes open to see Him? Am I listening for His voice?
3. Am I eager and prepared to participate when He invites me to join Him?
4. Am I standing my ground for Him where He has placed me?

That's what I want for myself, and that's what I want for you too. So keep reading and let's process this together. First, we'll examine the state of the church today and remember how God has used people in the past to accomplish His purposes. Then we'll reflect on the condition of our own hearts and consider the resources that are available to us. Finally, we'll think about the path going forward and the good things God has in store for us if we choose to follow Him.

A PRAYER AGAINST DECEPTION

Lord Jesus, forgive us. Forgive us for our pride and our rebellion. Forgive us for elevating ourselves and our will and our choices above Yours. We come to You in humility. Forgive us for any time we have sought direction or guidance from a source other than You. We renounce it. We repent of it. We choose a new path. I thank You that through the blood of Jesus we have been delivered, redeemed, and cleansed. Only You can keep us from deception. Only You can secure our future. Only You can chart a course that will lead us triumphantly through what is ahead. We trust You and invite You into our hearts and our lives as never before. Give us hearts to receive, ears to hear, and eyes to see. Give us new boldness, new courage, and a new authority. Thank You for Your Word. Give us a love for it that cannot be quenched. Thank You for Your great love for us and for Your provision for us. I know that You have good things ahead for us. In Jesus' name, amen.

A PROCLAMATION OF HOPE

Jesus is Lord over every pandemic. He is Lord over every government and every government official. Jesus is Lord over every organization. He is Lord over the media and all those who imagine they can control the flow of information. Jesus is Lord in our homes. Jesus is Lord of our future. He is the head of the church. He's the image of the invisible God, the firstborn of all creation. By Him all things were created, both in the heavens and on the earth, visible and invisible. Jesus is before all things, and in Him all things hold together. Those who are with Him are the called and chosen and faithful. Jesus is the faithful witness, the firstborn from the dead. He loves us, and He freed us from our sins by His blood. He has made us to be a kingdom of priests to serve His Father. To Him be glory forever and ever. Amen!

CHAPTER 2

THE CHURCH SHAKEN AND CHURCH EXPOSED

Each one should build with care. For no one can lay any foundation other than the one already laid, which is Jesus Christ.
—1 CORINTHIANS 3:10-11

I can say with confidence that most pastors in America never imagined that government at any level would ask churches to close their doors, as occurred in 2020. That is the kind of thing that persecuted believers in other countries experience!

For believers in America, this season brings to mind things like harassment, discrimination, and perhaps even persecution. The Pew Research Center described harassment because of religion with the broad terms "government restrictions" and "social hostilities."[1] Open Doors described Christian persecution as "any hostility experienced as a result of identification with Jesus Christ." No matter which words you use, the fact is that Christianity is experiencing intensifying persecution on a global scale. In the fifty countries where it is most difficult to be a Christian, 360 million Jesus followers experience high levels of persecution and discrimination.[2]

While the United States is not on that list, the government's recent intrusion into the life of the American church has been unprecedented and shocking. Churches across the country have faced restrictions on their meetings and ministries even as businesses opened and other groups gathered, including protesters by the thousands.

In Nevada, for example, the governor signed a law allowing casinos, movie theaters, bars, and many other businesses to open at 50 percent capacity but limited a house of worship to fifty people, no matter its size.[3] When Calvary Chapel Dayton Valley asked the US Supreme Court to strike down the fifty-person limit on houses of worship, the court rejected 5–4 the church's argument that the restriction was unconstitutional.

Justice Samuel Alito wrote in a dissent that the different standard was illogical: "The Constitution guarantees the free exercise of religion. It says nothing about the freedom to play craps or blackjack, to feed tokens into a slot machine or to engage in any other game of chance. But the governor of Nevada apparently has different priorities." His dissent was joined by Justices Clarence Thomas and Brett Kavanaugh.[4]

To say that the church in America has been shaken is an understatement.

HOW DID WE GET HERE?

I believe the forces that have contributed to the shaking have been building even as everything around us appeared to be calm. Paul advised us to build the church of Jesus Christ with care, but we haven't always been faithful to do that. One of the revelations of this season is that the church had been asleep for a very long time when we were violently awakened by the disruptions brought on by a global pandemic. We sat up, groggy, rubbing our eyes, and looking around at an unfamiliar landscape. How did we get here? How could our churches have been caught so unprepared?

The Idols of Comfort and Convenience

Comfort and convenience have become idols for Americans, and that includes us—the Christians who make up our churches. You wouldn't believe some of the comments I've heard about inconvenient worship times (we offer several each week), or how far away from the door someone had to park, or the aggravation of having to find another seat because a visitor sat in a regular attender's usual place. And those are just the tip of the iceberg!

I am humbled by the attitudes of believers in other parts of the world. When I preached at a Bible conference in Kenya, for example, pastors came from all over the region to sit for hours and hear the Word of God taught. The sanctuary was a tent with weathered holes in the roof. In one meeting, the guitar had two strings missing and the drums had no heads. Those things did not seem to hinder their enthusiasm and worship at all!

Following God has very little to do with comfort and convenience. When I read about Paul's ministry flourishing through so many hardships, and even while he was in prison, it seems that focusing on comfort and convenience has made us sluggish and ineffective.

We've wanted, in Dietrich Bonhoeffer's words, "cheap grace."[5] We've wanted an "easy believe-ism" that doesn't require

> **Following God has very little to do with comfort and convenience.**

much of us. Something that is based on convenience and comfort and ease of use. Something that will be there on Easter and Christmas, or when the weather isn't good for boating or golf, or there isn't some sporting event on television. I don't say this to hand you a sense of guilt or shame, but I don't think we can wake up and change our condition until we recognize the condition we are in.

I know that Jesus loves the American church. We wouldn't be where we are and experiencing so many blessings without His grace and mercy. But I also believe that He has allowed us to be shaken in order to sift us and purify us. I believe that He is asking each of us, "What are your priorities? Are you willing to do whatever it takes to follow Me? Are you prepared to make personal sacrifices and invest yourself here, in this congregation and this community? Are you prepared to do whatever is necessary to make it possible for more people to hear the good news about Me?"

Tolerance and Inclusion

One of the most insulting things you can be called today is intolerant, and one of the highest compliments you can be paid is to be called inclusive. That goes for individuals and all kinds of groups and organizations, including churches. I received my first lesson in this many years ago when I enrolled in the divinity school at a prestigious university. I was given two documents. The first said I must not reference God with a male pronoun or the title "Father." If I wrote it in a paper, I would receive a failing grade. If I spoke it, I'd be asked to be quiet. I was to use inclusive language, such as "Heavenly Parent."

The other document stated that tolerance was a core value of the institution and that they would be very intolerant if I wasn't tolerant. Incredibly, they didn't see any contradiction between those two positions! That respected institution still gives "consistent attention to the use of inclusive language, especially in relation to the Divine," as well as "providing safe space . . . for those who are transitioning from one gender to another."[6]

We shake our heads at the ironies of a distinguished theological school basing their teaching on unbiblical principles such as these, but it should be a wake-up call for the biblically orthodox in the American church. The people coming out of that institution and others like it are going into positions of ministry and leadership: pastors, youth ministers, counselors, social workers, denominational leaders, and more. The theology they are being taught is the theology they are taking into the world and using to shape churches and lives.

Spiritual Potluck

I would be remiss if I did not mention the spiritual potluck that passes for theology in many churches. Paul told the Galatians he was "astonished that you are so quickly deserting the one who called you to live in the grace of Christ and are turning to a different gospel" (Galatians 1:6). The gospel I see in many churches today has left behind the God of the Bible as its sole authority and reshaped itself to accommodate personal preferences—and that includes accommodating blatant sin. In addition, the steady creep of Eastern religions, New Age practices, secular humanism, and even the occult into our theology has weakened our defenses against the evil and deception running rampant in our world.

THE MISSING PIECE

The missing piece, of course, is the recognition that God wants us to deny ourselves and seek the holiness that He requires, because "without holiness no one will see the Lord" (Hebrews 12:14). And we cannot change God's definition of holiness based on our own spiritual condition, or even based on the most spiritual person we know, because every one of us is an imperfect sinner. God's standard is His own absolute holiness, and none of us comes close to that.

No matter what some people and churches would have you believe, God does not grade our holiness on a curve. I once went to the hospital to pray for a man who was facing a grave diagnosis and serious surgery the next day. I said, "I would be uncaring if I didn't ask you this. Are you ready in case the surgery doesn't go the way you hope it will? Are you prepared to meet God?"

This intelligent, successful man looked at me and said, "Well, I'm a whole lot better than the guy who lives across the street from me." I told him that I didn't doubt that, but unless the man across the street was God, it really didn't matter.

It is human nature to compare ourselves with others, but that is not helpful when we're talking about the righteousness of God. It cannot be gained by anything we do or don't do—even if we are "better than the guy across the street." It does not matter that you are a kinder person than your neighbor or coworker. It does not matter that you donate to worthwhile charities. It does not matter that you volunteer at your local food bank.

There is nothing we can do to earn God's righteousness. And no matter what anyone says, it's not "all good." "Go along and get along" is not what the Bible tells us to do. And as for "living your truth," it takes far more courage to live God's truth than to settle for the comfort of your own.

Each of us must come to the realization that no matter how good we think we are or how good we appear to the

> No matter how good we think we are or how good we appear to the world, we will never be good enough to save ourselves.

world, we will never be good enough to save ourselves. Salvation through the blood of Jesus is our only hope, and His righteousness can be our righteousness!

THREE UNCHANGING REALITIES

Jesus warned His disciples that the world would always push back against the three unchanging realities that define true religion: sin, righteousness, and judgment. Sin is rebellion against God, and it is a part of every person's carnal nature. Righteousness is the ability to stand before God without guilt or shame, and it is available only through Jesus. And God is our loving yet unchanging and uncompromising Judge. Jesus also said that when the Holy Spirit came, He would "prove the world to be in the wrong about sin and righteousness and judgment" (John 16:8).

Many in the contemporary church have reservations about presenting God as a judge because they fear that it will hurt attendance, but the leaders of the early church never hesitated to talk about Him in that way. When Peter went to the home of Cornelius and presented the good news about Jesus in a completely non-Jewish setting, he said that Jesus "commanded us to preach to the people and to testify that he is the one whom God appointed as judge of the living and the dead. All the prophets testify about him that everyone who believes in him receives forgiveness of sins through his name" (Acts 10:42–43). It's interesting that even before Peter told these nonbelievers that Jesus is the Savior of the world, he told them He is the "judge of the living and the dead." He wasn't the least bit concerned about the truth frightening them away!

Neither was Paul concerned with mincing words about the reality of God's judgment. He told the people of Athens, a Gentile city, "In the past God overlooked such ignorance, but now he commands all people everywhere to repent. For he has set a day when he will judge the world with justice by the man he has appointed" (Acts 17:30–31).

The New Testament tells us there will be two different judgments. There will be a judgment of eternal destiny for those who stand apart from the Lord, and there will be a judgment for believers where our lives will be assessed and our rewards given. Can you imagine what it will be like when we are called to stand in the presence of the King of kings and Lord of lords and have our lives reviewed? It is foolish for us to live as if that judgment will not happen. And it is cruel for us to be certain of that event but not tell others—those who have never trusted Jesus for their salvation, and those who call themselves Christians but have shaped God Almighty into a God who is all love and no judgment.

The Bible says that we are to be ambassadors for the kingdom of God. That means we have a responsibility to be advocates for the God of the Bible, as He is presented in the Bible, even if His role as judge and His standard of absolute holiness make us uncomfortable.

CHURCH ISN'T ESSENTIAL?

With the American church in this weakened condition, it is not surprising that when we were told we were not essential, many of us agreed. I was glad to see that some churches stood strong and found creative ways to worship and minister in the midst of constant disruptions and challenges. I was surprised and disappointed to see so many other churches meekly shutting down and waiting for the government to give them permission to meet again.

Frankly, it has been frustrating and disheartening to see the soft underbelly of the American church exposed in this way. When I spoke to public officials and asked why liquor stores in our town were considered "essential" and were allowed to remain open when the churches were not, their answer was surprising and disappointing. They said they couldn't close the liquor stores because people would break in to get what they wanted. How I wish they could have said that about the churches! It's obvious that many Christians in America—including pastors—don't see their congregation's worship and fellowship as vitally important to themselves, their families, their communities, and the world that surrounds us.[7]

Can you imagine telling those early church leaders in the book of Acts that they were not essential? That their calling was valid only when it was comfortable and convenient? Or that they should continue only when the government gave its stamp of approval? Can you imagine informing Peter and John that it was not essential for them to keep telling about Jesus of Nazareth, their Savior and friend? Or what about Paul, who used every opportunity to talk about his Lord? Was his ministry unessential—his evangelism, his mentoring, his writing?

We, the church, are the twenty-first-century edition of the book of Acts. Just as those first followers of Jesus were essential to God's plans and purposes, so are we. No matter what the government or any other public voice says or would have us believe, we are essential workers as we strengthen God's kingdom and advance His purposes in the world.

BROTHER, CAN YOU SPARE SOME SHADE?

For almost a year at World Outreach Church we worshiped outdoors. Our "outdoor sanctuary" is nothing more than a large parking area behind our buildings and away from the major highway that runs in front of our property. It has a slight uphill slope and creates a natural amphitheater.

Our church met in a tent before we had a building, and

conventional wisdom says that you should do your best to recreate an indoor space wherever you are. To me, that meant lining up all the folding chairs in rows on the white lines in the parking lot—socially distanced. We soon learned that families didn't necessarily want to sit that way, so we began placing them in small groups scattered around the space.

Line of sight is also very important when you're planning an event, so I asked the campus facilities team to cut down all the trees in that parking lot. These are not ancient oaks, but they were relatively mature and pretty trees. It was late in the week when I made that decision, and they said, "We can't get that done before this weekend, but it can be done before next weekend."

When we got out there and actually used the space, we realized that people didn't care a bit about their line of sight or social distancing. Many sat in our folding chairs, but many others had brought along their own more comfortable chairs. And while they were still keeping a safe distance, they were sitting wherever they pleased and wherever there was shade!

I laughed and thought about how shortsighted my Paul Bunyan decision was and how quickly I would have regretted it. I soon realized that people are happier when they can make a simple choice like deciding where to sit, and we put up another screen so that they could see just fine from those shady spots!

DID YOU BRING AN UMBRELLA?

Naturally, our biggest challenge in meeting outside was the weather. Summer days in Tennessee mean high temperatures, high humidity, and a frequent chance of rain. We have services on Wednesday, Saturday, and Sunday, and each of those days became a weather watch. We couldn't turn on the outside equipment if there was lightning within two miles, so the crew in the tech booth had a micro weather station to monitor. We learned that we really appreciated a little cloud cover, and we could tolerate a sprinkle. We just didn't want rain or lightning.

Saturday, August 1, 2020, is a day that will live large in my memories of World Outreach Church. As I was getting ready to walk onto the platform to preach that night, it began sprinkling a little bit. The tech crew looked at their weather station and told me, "We're going to have a little shower, but it won't be more than a couple of minutes. Don't worry. Everything will be fine."

Well, they should keep their day jobs because they probably wouldn't make it as weather forecasters! As I began speaking, it began to rain. I mean really rain. We had a big crowd that night, as big as we'd had all summer because we were supposed to have a concert afterward. The ones who had checked the weather forecast beforehand had come prepared. Some opened umbrellas, and some pulled on ponchos. The rest were getting soaked, but no one got up to leave.

I was standing on a covered stage, but soon I was dripping wet and wiping the rain out of my eyes. The rain had become a torrent, no longer just falling but now also being driven horizontally by the wind. My sermon notes were in a three-ring binder, but they were being whipped back and forth and were soon so soggy and the ink so smeared that I could barely read them.

I finally just had to stop and laugh at the situation. And then I had to stop and pray, "Lord, let righteousness rain down on us." My sermon—on spiritual warfare, by the way—got preached, but not quite according to the outline I had so carefully crafted. The Holy Spirit filled that outdoor sanctuary, the people were freed up from their usual polite constraints, and we had church!

We look back on it now with smiles and amazement that it happened the way it did. All of us who were there that night knew that the Lord had done something unusual in our midst, but it was just one of the many extraordinary experiences we had with the Holy Spirit that summer. "In 2019, you wouldn't have stayed in the rain for church," I said that night, to cheers from the crowd. "We're more desperate than we were a year ago. And we'll tell this story for a long time to come!"[8]

THE VALUE OF SHOWING UP

Any preacher learns to keep going through all kinds of distractions. But I'm humbly grateful to say that preaching outdoors has honed my ability to stay at least somewhat focused not only through driving rain but also through barking dogs, wailing sirens, roaring hot rods, and the rumble of construction equipment! I can tell you with absolute certainty that I will never again take meeting together for granted. And I will do everything in my power to make it happen—inside, outside, on a parking lot, in a field—wherever.

And I have never been more aware of the value of simply showing up. People give lip service to many things, but where they show up usually represents what they care about. We show up in all kinds of weather and sit on uncomfortable bleachers to support our children and our favorite teams. We show up for concerts, parades, dance recitals, and the county fair. Where we show up is a good indicator of our priorities in life.

So I encourage you to make the effort to show up and participate in the life of your church. Don't ever think that your presence doesn't matter; it does, to yourself and others. As you worship God, you will remind yourself of who He is, your beliefs about Him, your trust in Him, and your priorities. As you worship and serve, you will set an example for others. You will tangibly demonstrate that you are committed to growing spiritually and advancing the cause of Jesus Christ in the world.

> Where we show up is a good indicator of our priorities in life.

JESUS' WORDS TO SEVEN CHURCHES

It is good for us to remember that Jesus is intimately aware of everything that goes on in each of His churches on the earth. He knows when our aim is to please and glorify Him. And He knows when our aim is to please and glorify ourselves.

In Revelation 2–3, Jesus instructed John to write down specific messages to seven different congregations. In every message Jesus began with "I know" and went on to tell each church what He knew about them—their strengths, their weaknesses, their reputation, their hardships, their financial state, and more. Here's a very brief summary of what Jesus had to say to these groups of believers.

To the church in Ephesus. Jesus said that He knew their

deeds, their hard work, and their perseverance. He knew that they could not tolerate wicked people and had tested the claims of false teachers. He commended them for their perseverance and for enduring hardship for His name without growing weary. Yet He held it against them that their love for Him had dimmed from what it had been at first, and He wanted them to repent and regain their passion.

To the church in Smyrna. Jesus told them that He knew about their afflictions and their poverty but that they were rich in His eyes. He knew that they were suffering persecution for His sake and that they would suffer still more. He assured them, however, that no matter what they were asked to suffer for Him, He would reward them for it.

To the church in Pergamum. Jesus acknowledged that even though their city was a seat of Satanic power, they had stayed true to Him . . . mostly. He noted that some among them were following pagan teachings, and the rest of the group evidently had allowed them to remain in the fellowship without consequence. He instructed them to repent.

To the church in Thyatira. Jesus commended them for their deeds, their love and faith, their service and perseverance, and for increasing in those things. But some among them were tolerating a prophetess who was encouraging sexual immorality and other pagan practices. He encouraged any who sinned with her to repent, or they would face His punishment.

To the church in Sardis. Jesus acknowledged their deeds and something else: they had a reputation of being alive, but they were dead. They had done what many modern churches do—create a facade of activity that covers a spiritually dead congregation. Jesus had not given up on them, however, and He encouraged them to wake up and strengthen what remained.

To the church in Philadelphia. Jesus had given this congregation a special opportunity for evangelism, and He wanted them to take advantage of it. He acknowledged that while they had little strength of their own, His strength was sufficient for the task. And because they had endured patiently under persecution, He would spare them from the trial that would come on the whole earth in the future.

To the church in Laodicea. This congregation had convinced themselves that they were okay. They thought that because they were financially stable they didn't need anything else. But Jesus did not agree. He said that spiritually they were lukewarm, wretched, pitiful, poor, blind, and naked. He offered them remedies for their spiritual ills and famously asked to be invited into their lives.

WHAT ABOUT MY CHURCH... AND YOURS?

Jesus sent these messages to seven specific congregations, but He also intended them for "whoever has ears" to hear (Revelation 3:22). Jesus told every church, "I know your deeds." We can be assured that He knows everything our churches are doing—and not doing—as well as our motivations. So let's think about our churches, your church and my church, and consider what we are doing in light of Jesus' messages for the seven churches of Revelation.

1. Are we excited about our relationship with Jesus and about serving Him? Can the world see our excitement?

2. Are we working hard on His behalf and persevering when we face trials and hardships?

3. Would you say that your church is spiritually hot, cold, or lukewarm?

4. Do we depend on our financial resources for our spiritual security?

5. Is the God of the Bible our sole authority? Or have we allowed any unbiblical philosophies to infiltrate our fellowship?

6. Do we tolerate any false teachers in our congregation, or do we work to convince them of the truth of the gospel? If they will not be convinced, what do we do?

7. Do we tolerate sexual immorality of any kind?

8. Do we avoid doing anything that might cause us to suffer for the name of Jesus?

9. Have we created a facade of spiritual activity to cover a spiritually dead congregation?

10. Are we taking advantage of every open door for evangelism?

WHAT WILL BE SAID ABOUT US?

I often wonder what will be said about the church in this generation. We have stood by as prayer and the Ten Commandments have been removed from public places. We have failed to intervene while millions of babies have been killed through abortion. We were largely silent while pornography and violence became mainstream entertainment. We looked away while gender became a choice and the family was redefined. We accepted the government's declaration that church was not essential. We've allowed our worship to be dictated by comfort and convenience.

Now we see God shaking the things around us. What will our response be? Rather than being filled with panic and dread, we should allow our righteousness to shine. We should consider the source of our hope and our joy. We should allow the Holy Spirit to give us godly wisdom that we can share with others. We should share the hope found in the shed blood of Jesus and His righteousness.

This may seem like a tall order, but it is actually rather simple. It is simply living to honor the Lord . . . one day, one decision, and one conversation at a time.

CHAPTER 3

THE POWER OF ONE

For just as through the disobedience of the one man the many were made sinners, so also through the obedience of the one man the many will be made righteous.

—ROMANS 5:19

One person can make a difference for good.

That's a biblical principle that we see demonstrated throughout the Old and New Testaments and even today. Sometimes that difference will be obvious in the moment. Sometimes we can see the difference only in the rearview mirror of history and hindsight. And sometimes our days on earth will end without us seeing any difference at all, but it will be felt by the generations who follow us.

THE FIRST ADAM AND SECOND ADAM

The Bible talks about a first Adam and a second Adam who made choices that will be felt for eternity. We meet the first Adam in Genesis 1:27. I don't believe the Bible's account of Adam is a metaphorical story to introduce us to the concept of sin. I believe that Adam, the first human being created by God, rebelled and attempted to orchestrate a change of authority over all humanity. He wanted to be like God, so he took the bait that Satan offered.

Romans 5:12 says, "Therefore, just as sin entered the world through one man, and death through sin, and in this way death came to all people, because all sinned." This describes the battle with Satan and his kingdom of darkness that Adam engaged and every one of us faces on a daily basis, even after we make a profession of faith in Jesus. Even Jesus, the incarnate, perfectly obedient Son of God, was tempted by Satan. So it's naive to think that we are beyond temptation, that we have achieved such a level of heightened spirituality that Satan won't challenge the authority of God in our lives and invite us to rebel against Him.

Because of our rebellion against God, the second Adam stepped into time in a stable in Bethlehem. His name is Jesus, and He came to save us when we were powerless to save ourselves. One man took away our authority in the kingdom, and another Man made it possible again. Just as the result of one trespass was condemnation for all people, the result of one act of righteousness was justification that brings life for all people. Romans 5:17 says, "For if, by the trespass of the one man, death reigned through that one man, how much more will those who receive God's abundant provision of grace and of the gift of righteousness reign in life through the one man, Jesus Christ!" The unique, essential role of Jesus should never be forgotten or diminished. Redemption was accomplished

> **The unique, essential role of Jesus should never be forgotten or diminished.**

by One and made way for our participation in God's kingdom.

GOD IS LOOKING AND LISTENING FOR HIS PEOPLE

> So justice is driven back, and righteousness
> stands at a distance; truth has stumbled
> in the streets, honesty cannot enter.
> Truth is nowhere to be found, and whoever
> shuns evil becomes a prey.
> The Lord looked and was displeased that
> there was no justice. He saw that there
> was no one, he was appalled that
> there was no one to intervene. (Isaiah
> 59:14–16)

This passage could be taken from today's headlines. Justice and righteousness seem very far away. Truth has stumbled in the street and is being trampled underfoot. For many, honesty is an unwelcome enemy. If you stand for a biblical worldview and righteousness as presented in Scripture, you will be widely mocked. If you decide not to participate in evil, and you call it such, you will become a target.

When God saw this circumstance and was not pleased with it, He began to look for help from His people. He was astonished that no one was willing to intervene. These were His covenant people. They had a temple where they offered daily sacrifices, and their lives were filled with religious activity. But few voices were willing to speak against injustice and evil.

I'm sure they had many reasons that seemed sensible to them. Perhaps standing up for truth and righteousness would have meant bucking the status quo. Perhaps it would have meant losing friends, or social standing, or even work and income. If so, that was a shortsighted view, because God has always abundantly blessed anyone who is willing to stand up for Him.

> When I shut up the heavens so that there is no rain, or command locusts to devour the land or send a plague among my people, if my people, who are called by my name, will humble themselves and pray and seek my face and turn from their wicked ways, then I will hear from heaven, and I will forgive their sin and will heal their land. (2 Chronicles 7:13–14)

You probably know this verse, but you may not know the context. God was speaking to Solomon at the dedication of the temple in Jerusalem. This was the first time God had been willing to identify with a building constructed by human hands, so this magnificent structure was a symbol of God's abiding presence in the midst of His people. God used this momentous occasion, when He had the people's focused attention, to make this "when-if-then" declaration.

When I shut up the heavens so that there is no rain, or command locusts to devour the land or send a plague among my people. (v. 13)

Most of the people lived off the land, and their economy depended on growing crops and raising livestock. They understood the devastation God was describing if He caused their resources to evaporate through withholding rain or sending locusts or a plague.

If my people, who are called by my name, will humble themselves and pray and seek my face and turn from their wicked ways. (v. 14)

This is the dividing line in the passage, the determining factor between "when" and "then." God said, "What my people do will determine the outcome. Will they be willing to humble themselves and pray? Will they seek My face and turn from their wickedness?" These are the attitudes and behaviors God was looking for when He spoke it three thousand years ago, and they are the attitudes and behaviors He is still looking for today.

Then I will hear from heaven, and I will forgive their sin and will heal their land. (v. 14)

And here's the "then." If we will meet the conditions God has stated, then He will hear us, forgive us, and heal our land. What would it mean for God to heal our land? A land restored by God would be a place that is the very opposite of what Isaiah described above: Justice would be welcomed, and righteousness would be at the heart of our society. Truth would be honored, and honesty would be the benchmark for our conversation. Those who shun evil would be respected and held up as role models. What a glorious land that would be!

Like me, you may have been in a group that was asked to say this passage aloud as a prayerful declaration. We may feel sincere earnestness in our own hearts and see it in the faces around us. But how often have we truly taken the "If . . . then" of God's promise to heart? How often have we actually done the things that will bring God's forgiveness and blessing—humbling ourselves, praying, seeking His face, and turning from our ungodliness? How often have we prayed those things for other people but thought we ourselves were exempt from the need for humility and repentance? The challenges before us are not the result of the depravity of the wicked, but the indifference of the faithful.

It is time to allow the Holy Spirit to peel off our hardened layers and soften our hearts toward the Lord. It is time for us to be more concerned about repenting than trying to excuse or cover up our sin. It is time for us to fall on our faces in humility. It is time for us to be more interested in pursuing the things of God than the things of this world.

GOD WORKS THROUGH HIS PEOPLE

A principle found throughout Scripture is that God works through His people. It doesn't matter how perverse the culture becomes; what matters is how committed to holiness the church becomes. And that means each one of us, individually and collectively. God's people are the key, the difference makers, so we should stop bemoaning the power of the ungodly. God's people have always been, and will always be, at the center of His purposes.

If you look at God's people throughout the story of Scripture, you see that they were triumphant and victorious in generation after generation. But they were also frequently disregarded, over-matched, and outnumbered.

God at Work in the Old Testament

> David said to Saul, "Your servant has been keeping his father's sheep. When a lion or a bear came and carried off a sheep from the flock, I went after it, struck it and rescued the sheep from its mouth. When it turned on me, I seized it by its hair, struck it and killed it. Your servant has killed both the lion and the bear; this uncircumcised Philistine will be like one of them, because he has defied the armies of the living God. (1 Samuel 17:34–36)

Goliath had been taunting the Israelite army for forty days, challenging them to hand-to-hand combat, but not one of them was willing to take on the giant Philistine. Young David had brought food to the camp for his soldier brothers when Goliath stepped out and bellowed his challenge once again. David was angry at the insult to his God and said confidently to King Saul, "I can take him."

When Saul pointed out his youth, David shared his fighting credentials. The Israelite army may have had a whole squadron of stone-slingers, but none of them wanted anything to do with Goliath. Meanwhile, David had been tending sheep, and the challenges that went along with that humble task had prepared him for a future of serving God in bigger ways. Now, armed with a sling and five stones, he was determined to defend the name of his God—and the rest is history.

Experience with God is a very powerful tool. As a shepherd, David had honed his fighting skills in order to protect his flock, and that separated him from a whole army of trained warriors. He said, "God delivered those predators into my hand, and God will deliver this predator into my hand." God put a young shepherd boy in the path of a giant warrior, but He also provided him with five smooth stones and the skill to use them.

> "Pardon me, my lord," Gideon replied, "but how can I save Israel? My clan is the weakest in Manasseh, and I am the least in my family." The LORD answered, "I will be with you, and you will strike down all the Midianites, leaving none alive." (Judges 6:15–16)

Gideon is perhaps best known for leading a group of Israelite soldiers to defeat a much larger Midianite army. But when God first called Gideon, he was an ordinary young man doing chores on his father's farm. He certainly didn't feel as if the Lord was with him in any special way. Gideon was reluctant to believe that God would actually want to use him—his family were idol worshipers, after all! It took supernatural intervention to convince him that he was more than an insignificant person from an insignificant group of people.

God knew that drastic measures were necessary in order to keep Israel from boasting about their own strength, so God cut the young leader's army from thirty-two thousand men to a force of three hundred. And I can just imagine the expressions on their faces when they learned that their weapons would be trumpets, clay pots, and torches! Gideon had to keep taking some big steps of faith in order to understand that if God invited him to participate, He would take care of the details.

When God called Gideon, it was a pretty disruptive invitation. But after his initial reluctance, Gideon listened to God's instructions and arrived at the right place with the right group of people who were equipped in the right way for a victory that changed the course of the nation.

The Old Testament tells of many others whom God used in spite of their imperfect stories or their hesitation. Moses was a murderer who had fled to the desert to escape the death penalty when God called him to lead His people out of slavery. Joseph's brothers sold him into slavery, but he rose to a position of great power and eventually kept them and their families from starving during a famine. Esther was a beautiful young woman who concealed her Jewish identity in order to become the queen of Persia, then used her position to save her people from destruction. Daniel was enslaved from his youth, yet God favored him, and we still look to his faithfulness as an example.

God at Work in the New Testament

The New Testament begins another chapter in the unfolding story of God's interactions with people. The time and the context differ from the Old Testament, but we still see God using a host of very different individuals to advance His kingdom purposes.

In those days John the Baptist came, preaching in the wilderness of Judea and saying, "Repent, for the kingdom of heaven has come near." . . . John's clothes were made of camel's hair, and he had a leather belt around his waist. His food was locusts and wild honey. (Matthew 3:1–2, 4)

We know John the Baptist as the desert-dwelling forerunner of Jesus, and we tend to read past him to get to the hero of the story. But God used John to bring many people to repentance. He is best known for baptizing Jesus, but untold numbers of other people came from the surrounding region to be baptized by him in the Jordan River.

John was always quick to deflect attention away from himself and toward the coming Messiah, whom he eagerly awaited: "But after me comes one who is more powerful than I, whose sandals I am not worthy to carry. He will baptize you with the Holy Spirit and fire" (Matthew 3:11). John's message got the attention of the power brokers in Jerusalem, and King Herod had him arrested because John had criticized the king's affair with his brother's wife. John was eventually beheaded because of his stand for righteousness.

But John's story began many years before. The angel Gabriel had appeared to John's father, Zechariah, to say that his prayers had been answered and his wife would bear a son. The child, whom they were to name John, would "be filled with the Holy Spirit even before he is born. He will bring back many of the people of Israel to the Lord their God. And he will go on before the Lord, in the spirit and power of Elijah, to turn the hearts of the parents to their children and the disobedient to the wisdom of the righteous—to make ready a people prepared for the Lord" (Luke 1:15–17). Zechariah and Elizabeth were very old, so this was both a surprise and a miracle. Before John was even conceived, God had a plan for his life, and John was faithful to fulfill it.

God also worked through Peter, who had come a long way from where we first met him—a young fisherman hauling in his nets, a faithful but ordinary Jewish man waiting for the Messiah along with the rest of his people. Since then he had spent time with Jesus, watching and learning. He had seen miracles and even demonstrated enough faith to walk on water.

But Peter's ministry was not all smooth sailing. Peter was a passionate man, and sometimes he allowed his emotions to get the best of him. Once, in defense of Jesus, he cut a man's ear off with a sword. Not long after that event, he did the very opposite and denied his Lord—three times! Sometime later, in a theological dustup known as the Incident at Antioch, Paul had to rebuke him publicly because Peter wouldn't stand up to the Judaizers, the people who kept insisting on adhering to Jewish traditions (Galatians 2:11–20). Peter was called by the Lord to make a difference for His kingdom, but sometimes he buckled under the pressure.

One of the things we can learn from Peter is that good people, godly people, don't always have absolute clarity about what to do. And sometimes we allow ourselves to be led by our emotions. That's not due to any particular failure within us; we are just imperfect people who are predisposed to drift. It is part of the human condition and a challenge we all face. The pressures to veer off the path are real, and they're disorienting. We don't want to accept spiritual sloppiness, but we've got to acknowledge these tendencies in ourselves and say, "Okay, how do we minimize and shore up these weak spots?" That's why we've got to stay grounded through Bible reading, prayer, and living in community with other believers. We need all of those things to keep us on a godly path.

> Christ Jesus came into the world to save sinners—of whom I am the worst. But for that very reason I was shown mercy so that in me, the worst of sinners, Christ Jesus might display his immense patience as an example for those who would believe in him and receive eternal life. (1 Timothy 1:15–16)

This was a complete change of heart and direction for the man who had hunted down and executed anyone who suggested that Jesus was the Messiah. As a younger man, Paul had been the rising star of the religious establishment. He had the right family background, the right education, and the right connections. After Jesus got his attention by throwing him in the dust and temporarily blinding him, Paul refocused his intellect and his drive and began to preach the very message that he had so fervently persecuted others for sharing.

After Paul decided to serve the Lord, he was thrown out of as many places as he was welcomed. Almost everywhere he went to preach, there was a riot or some other public expression of displeasure. He was given thirty-nine lashes five times (forty were supposed to kill a man) and surely would have been physically disfigured by the scar tissue from those beatings. He was shipwrecked and spent multiple days and nights on the open sea. Most of us, myself included, would have been reluctant to travel with him!

Paul was as zealous on behalf of Jesus as he had been in opposition to Him. No matter what physical challenge or opposition he faced, he refused to stop. He simply moved to the next place and began to talk about Jesus again. Because of his devotion and perseverance in evangelism and discipleship, Paul is considered the most effective ambassador for the kingdom of God that our world has ever known.

> After this, Paul left Athens and went to Corinth. There he met a Jew named Aquila, a native of Pontus, who had recently come from Italy with his wife Priscilla, because Claudius had ordered all Jews to leave Rome. Paul went to see them, and because he was a tentmaker as they were, he stayed and worked with them. . . .
>
> . . . Meanwhile a Jew named Apollos, a native of Alexandria, came to Ephesus. He was a learned man, with a thorough knowledge of the Scriptures. He had been instructed in the way of the Lord, and he spoke with great fervor and taught about Jesus accurately, though he knew only the baptism of John. He began to speak boldly in the synagogue. When Priscilla and Aquila heard him, they invited him to their home and explained to him the way of God more adequately. (Acts 18:1–3, 24–26)

Aquila and Priscilla are two of the lesser-known stars of the New Testament. Paul first met them in Corinth, where they were living after the Roman emperor had driven the Jewish population out of Rome. They were believers and tentmakers like Paul, so he lived and worked with them. The three of them may have been the first small group based on shared interests—and what a productive small group they were!

Paul eventually decided it was time to leave Corinth, and Aquila and Priscilla went with him. When their ship made a stop in Ephesus, they stayed there to minister in that community while Paul went on. When a fiery preacher named Apollos came to Ephesus, they took him in and "explained to him the way of God more adequately." It's worth noting that Apollos was awakening people to the story of Jesus while he himself was still learning about Jesus. We don't tell the Jesus-story because we have all the answers; we learn about Jesus while we are serving Him. That is true for all of us.

To the Corinthians Paul wrote, "Aquila and Priscilla greet you warmly in the Lord, and so does the church that meets at their house" (1 Corinthians 16:19). By the time he wrote to the Romans, the couple was back in that city. "Greet Priscilla and Aquila, my co-workers in Christ Jesus. They risked their lives for me. Not only I but all the churches of the Gentiles are grateful to them. Greet also the church that meets at their house" (Romans 16:3–5).

Aquila and Priscilla were part of a group of ordinary individuals who believed that Jesus of Nazareth was the Messiah and demonstrated that belief through their actions. This single-minded couple yielded their lives completely to the cause of Christ. They worked together and traveled together. They opened their homes to other believers and even started churches in their homes. The places where they served may have shifted a bit, but their purpose never wavered. They simply oriented every aspect of their lives around taking the Jesus-story to one place and then the next.

God at Work in You

But you are a chosen people, a royal priesthood, a holy nation, God's special possession, that you may declare the praises of

him who called you out of darkness into his wonderful light.
(1 Peter 2:9)

Do you believe that God chose you to be a royal priest of His holy nation? He did! And you are! You are "God's special possession"—not so that you can hang your baptismal certificate on the wall and declare your business with God done, but so that you can declare His praises to the world. That doesn't mean being religious or keeping a set of rules. That means we are so grateful that He has called us out of the darkness and into His light that we want to say yes to His invitations. We are so eager to share the good news about His light-filled kingdom that we are willing to have our plans disrupted.

It would be nice to think that when God told Noah to build an ark, Noah thought, "Yes! I'll get to use all my tools!" I don't really believe that. I think that Noah was a normal person who sincerely loved God, but I also think he probably had some serious questions along the way. We sometimes project onto others a spiritual ease that we don't feel in order to excuse our own hesitation. There are several reasons for that, but I think that many of us simply feel unqualified and unequipped to do the tasks God has set before us.

Jesus has invited me many times to leave my comfort zone and trust Him in new ways.

Jesus has invited me many times to leave my comfort zone and trust Him in new ways. Every time I have said yes to Him, He has expanded my horizons beyond any dream or goal I ever had. For every one of us, our future holds great promise and potential, and it begins by believing that Jesus has greater plans for us than we can even imagine.

The good news is that our God is faithful. He will give us everything we need in order to do what He invites us to do. God has always equipped ordinary people to do extraordinary things, and we are no different. But we have to admit that we are human, and we struggle with obstacles in our path—both real and imagined. Perhaps we have seen Christians who suffered consequences for following Jesus publicly. Perhaps we wonder if we will be rejected by family members. Perhaps we believe that our job opportunities will be diminished. Perhaps we fear that we will no longer be welcome in our social circles.

From decades of life and ministry, I have observed that many people will sell their future in order to be accepted by someone whose approval they value more than that of the Lord. They have hidden what they say they believe and mortgaged their integrity in order to get along, get ahead, and not bring division.

We've rationalized those decisions by telling ourselves we're protecting friendships, or opportunities for our children, or our future financial needs, or family unity. No matter the excuse we've given ourselves, the reality is that we've dimmed the light that Jesus expects us to shine into the darkness.

I love to study and learn, and in my younger years I was in more than one academic setting where the truth about Jesus was marginalized or unwelcome. Sometimes I turned down the volume on my beliefs in order to get through a class without making too much of a commotion, and I regret that. Now my objective is to consistently acknowledge that Jesus is God's Son. I believe that He was conceived by the Holy Spirit and born of a virgin named Mary. I believe that He lived a sinless life among us and was crucified on a Roman cross for our sins. I believe that He rose from the dead and is at the right hand of His Father's throne. And I believe that He will return someday to judge the living and the dead.

As a follower of Jesus, your life is no longer your own. If you're still thinking of your days in terms of my life, my time, my goals, and my money, you haven't really grappled with what it means to be a Christ follower. The Bible says that when we follow Jesus, we forfeit our self-determination and offer ourselves to Him as living sacrifices. That means living according to a new set of priorities that don't begin with "I." Jesus said, "Whoever wants to be my disciple must deny themselves and take up their cross and follow me" (Matthew 16:24). That doesn't mean just once at an altar when you say the sinner's prayer; that means every day.

God invites each of His children to be aware of their kingdom destiny. You are on earth for a reason—that God's kingdom will come and His will be done through you. No matter your age, your background, your education, or your current circumstances, God has a place and a purpose for you. Don't ever lose sight of that.

And He has not left you alone to figure this out with your own reasoning and intellect. He has given you His Spirit to help you understand where you fit into His plan. If you will lean into that relationship with your whole heart, mind, soul, and body, the rewards for you will exceed anything you can imagine.

DON'T BE LEFT BEHIND

Shortly before dawn Jesus went out to them, walking on the lake. When the disciples saw him walking on the lake, they were terrified. "It's a ghost," they said, and cried out in fear. But Jesus immediately said to them: "Take courage! It is I. Don't be afraid." "Lord, if it's you," Peter replied, "tell me to come to you on the water." "Come," he said. (Matthew 14:25–29)

I'll close this chapter with one final scene from the Gospels. I want you to imagine the disciples crossing the Sea of Galilee late one moonlit night. These were familiar waters, and they were naturally terrified when they saw a man walking toward their boat. When Jesus identified Himself to calm their fears, Peter spoke up and made one of the most famous requests in the Bible: "Lord, if it's really You, tell me to come to You on the water." And what was Jesus' response? "Come on!"

We usually hear this story as an example of Peter's trust in Jesus that surged, then faltered: "Then Peter got down out of the boat, walked on the water and came toward Jesus. But when he saw the wind, he was afraid and, beginning to sink, cried out, 'Lord, save me!' Immediately Jesus reached out his hand and caught him. 'You of little faith,' he said, 'why did you doubt?'" (vv. 29–31).

But instead of Peter, who showed at least a little faith, I'd like for you to think about the other men in that boat. Think about the ones who didn't ask to go to Jesus, the ones who never got out of the boat and never got their feet wet. Why did they keep quiet? Why did they stay in their seats? Because they didn't think, or at least they weren't sure, that Jesus had the power to bring them across the waves. What were they thinking as Peter stepped out and started walking? Were they embarrassed that their lack of faith had been revealed? Were they filled with regret that they hadn't asked too?

I have a challenge for each one of us as we close this section

THE POWER OF ONE

and consider how God might use us in the world. Let's not be the ones who stay behind in the safety and security of the boat. Let's be the ones who step out and get our feet wet. Let's be the ones who trust Jesus to do the miraculous.

SOME THINGS TO THINK ABOUT

1. David used one of the skills he had learned while defending a flock of sheep to defeat an enemy of God's people. What skills do you have that could be used to advance God's purposes on the earth?

2. Gideon felt insignificant and couldn't understand how God could use him, but he said yes to God's invitation and plan. Do you ever feel insignificant and unworthy of a role in God's kingdom? What has God said about your worth and your significance?

3. John the Baptist lived very simply in order to fulfill God's plan for him. Have you ever intentionally simplified your lifestyle in order to free up more time or resources for God's purposes?

4. Like Peter, you are in process and will make some mistakes. Have you invited God into your days and asked Him to fill you with His Holy Spirit? Are you intentionally stretching your spiritual muscles and learning what it means to be used by Him?

5. Paul faced constant hardship and challenges during his years as an advocate for the Lord. What does that tell us we should expect in our assignment as ambassadors for Jesus of Nazareth?

6. Aquila and Priscilla were a married couple who worked and ministered together. If you are married, what example does this set for your life together as a couple?

7. God asked Noah to begin building a massive ark before anyone of his generation had seen a flood. Have you ever said yes to one of God's invitations when you didn't have all the details or it didn't seem logical in your eyes? What was the result?

8. Think about Peter stepping out of the boat and walking across the water to meet Jesus. Do you have the faith of Peter? Or do you have the faith of the men in the boat?

CHAPTER 4

FUNDAMENTALS MATTER

Do your best to present yourself to God as one approved, a worker who does not need to be ashamed and who correctly handles the word of truth.

—2 TIMOTHY 2:15

Fundamentals matter—always have, always will.

Swish! Can you name the best free-throw shooter in the world? You might be surprised to know that it is Bob Fisher, a sixty-something soil conservation technician from Centralia, Kansas. Fisher is no basketball superstar, just a guy who played high school and rec league basketball and decided several years ago that he would start practicing free throws every day.[1] Today he is the world's fastest shooter and the holder of many other Guinness World Records, including shooting with alternating hands and while blindfolded.[2]

"My pleasure!" For several years Chick-fil-A has made

innovation and top-notch customer service a priority. While their innovation leads to behind-the-scenes improvements, their commitment to friendly and attentive customer service has led to brand loyalty that no other quick-service restaurant enjoys. During the COVID-19 pandemic, when inefficiency created confusion and frustration at some drive-thru vaccination sites, who was called in to help? Chick-fil-A managers![3]

"It's too hot!" After watching several construction projects on our church property, I've learned the value of a good load of concrete. Every truckload that is poured is sampled and put through tests for temperature, air content, density, yield, and other measurable standards. If any of those tests reveal a subpar mix, that load is taken up and a new one is brought in. The construction industry has learned to take care of these things on the front end to minimize losses on the back end. No matter how beautiful the structure being built, it's not going to stand the test of time if you don't get the foundation right.[4]

THE NECESSITY OF A GOOD FOUNDATION

Jesus told a parable about how that same principle applies to the importance of a good foundation in our spiritual lives. We've heard the parable of the two builders so many times that I'm afraid we don't pay much attention to it or think it's just a clever story for children. But it is vitally important for believers to understand its message and take it to heart.

As for everyone who comes to me and hears my words and
puts them into practice, I will show you what they are like.

They are like a man building a house, who dug down deep and laid the foundation on rock. When a flood came, the torrent struck that house but could not shake it, because it was well built. But the one who hears my words and does not put them into practice is like a man who built a house on the ground without a foundation. The moment the torrent struck that house, it collapsed and its destruction was complete. (Luke 6:47–49)

Picture two houses built for two families. They look identical in every way and sit on adjoining lots. The only way you can tell the difference is by looking at the house numbers. They are lovely inside and out, the dream home of each family. Then one day a storm passes through, and each house takes the same direct hit. One is destroyed, and the family is left to sift through the rubble. The other is missing a few shingles and a shutter is dangling, but the family and their possessions sit undisturbed inside.

Each house was subjected to the same storm, but one factor determined two very different outcomes: One builder didn't worry too much about the quality of the foundation or about securely attaching the frame to it. The other builder went to great lengths to ensure that the foundation was strong and deep and that the frame was firmly attached.

We are living in a time of fierce storms, and you may feel like your house has taken a direct hit. Jesus said there is only one way to keep from being reduced to rubble, and that is by hearing what He says and doing it. This is not complicated or beyond our understanding. The most stabilizing thing you can do is know the Word of God and do what it says. Anything else you invest yourself in or attach yourself to will eventually take a direct hit and be destroyed.

Realize this, though. Being a believer in Jesus of Nazareth will not protect you from being subjected to the storms of life. In fact, quite the opposite is often true. The pressure on Jesus' disciples went up exponentially after they were baptized in the Spirit. They weren't threatened, arrested, or beaten until after that event. But that also is when they were empowered to go into the world and make a difference for God's kingdom.

> God allows us to be exposed to pressures in order to increase our understanding of His character.

God allows us to be exposed to pressures in order to increase our understanding of His character. As we face the storms that life brings, we are refined and more accurately reflect the image of our Savior. And in that process, we become more useful for Him.

BACK TO THE BASICS

The famous NFL coach Vince Lombardi died many years ago, but his motivational statements live on. One of my favorites is his reminder to the Green Bay Packers on the first day of training camp: "Gentlemen, this is a football." Lombardi was speaking to grown men, professionals, many of whom had played the sport since childhood. He wasn't trying to embarrass or humiliate them. He simply wanted to impress upon them that the key to victory was mastering the fundamentals. He wanted the basic skills of football to be honed to a high level and become second nature so that the players would do them without thinking during a game—and his record of success proved that his coaching strategy was a good one.[5]

We in the American church have been so affluent and so sheltered from the world's storms that we have not needed to cultivate the fundamental skills of our faith. We have depended on our ability to manage our lives, to earn a living and protect ourselves from life's disruptions. But our world is changing, and we need to develop a new confidence in the Lord and our relationship with Him.

That will require us to think about the fundamentals of our faith in a new way. We need to be willing to humble ourselves and admit that we may have made a profession of faith, but the faith we profess is not very deep. It is time for us to get back to the basics and open our lives to the involvement of God.

I have found that the best way to master the fundamentals of Christianity is to intentionally cultivate a desire to know more about God and to become closer to Him. I can do that by consistently reading my Bible and committing myself to prayer. In challenging seasons, it is enormously helpful to know what God has said in His Word—about Himself, about me, about my days on the earth, and about my future. And it is reassuring to know that in spite of all my weaknesses, almighty God, the Creator of the universe and everything in it, wants to have a relationship with me based on honest communication.

Getting Started with Daily Bible Reading

The Bible is God's good gift to us, and it is a transformative thing when we read it and apply it to our lives. It may have

"Holy" printed on the cover, but I am not suggesting that you worship the book; I am encouraging you to give it a unique place of authority in your life.

I believe the Bible is completely true and authoritative, but it is not a complete presentation of all God has ever done or will do. Its central theme is the spiritual welfare of humanity, and if you're interested in your own personal transformation—body, soul, and spirit—then the Word of God is the best resource I know. Invest time in it, and you will begin to see God's purposes fulfilled in you and through you.

We will talk more about the Bible in the next chapter. Right now, I want to simply encourage you to read it. There are multiple plans for reading your Bible systematically that are available online and in print formats. You can choose to read it from beginning to end, Genesis 1 to Revelation 22. You can choose to read it chronologically. You can listen to an audio version. You can combine your Bible reading with your prayer time. You can use a journal to record your thoughts, prayers, and praises.

People often ask me which Bible translation is the best, and my answer is predictable: the best translation is the one you'll read! Some translations use simpler words. Some have more contemporary language. Some were translated from the original languages one word at a time. Others were translated one phrase or sentence at a time. Some Bibles include maps and other study aids that can be very helpful. The important thing is to find one you're comfortable with and start reading.

One of the best things we've done as a church in the last several years is make a commitment to systematically read our Bibles on a daily basis. We vary our Bible reading plan from year to year, but each plan takes us through the entire Bible in one year. I have seen many examples of how God has honored our willingness and perseverance and blessed us as individuals, families, and as a congregation. We have devoted a page on our website to that year's schedule.[6] You also can listen to an audio version on one of our apps. However and wherever you choose to partake of God's Word, jump in!

Learning to Pray

This, then, is how you should pray:

> "Our Father in heaven,
> hallowed be your name,
> your kingdom come,
> your will be done, on earth as it is in heaven.
> Give us today our daily bread.
> And forgive us our debts, as we also have
> forgiven our debtors.
> And lead us not into temptation, but deliver us
> from the evil one."

> For if you forgive other people when they sin against you, your heavenly Father will also forgive you. But if you do not forgive others their sins, your Father will not forgive your sins. (Matthew 6:9–15)

Jesus prayed to His Father, and He wanted us to learn to pray too. This prayer, known as the Lord's Prayer, is probably the most repeated prayer in the world. I imagine that you have recited it alone and in groups many times. Jesus gave a very similar response on another occasion when one of His disciples said to

Him, "Lord, teach us to pray" (Luke 11:1–4). I imagine that they had watched Jesus pray many times. They knew that there was something different about the way He prayed, and they wanted that for themselves.

This prayer is simple and brief. Jesus had already cautioned them about trying to impress anyone—themselves, any listeners, or even their heavenly Father—with lots of words (Matthew 6:7). But He packed a great deal into what He did say. These few verses are so rich with meaning that Jesus didn't give us just one prayer, He gave us a whole portfolio of prayers. Let's look at the different components of what is sometimes called the model prayer.

"Our Father in heaven." Note that He didn't say "My" Father, but "our" Father. Every person who follows Jesus is included in God's family. There is no distinction made due to your place of birth, your ethnicity, your age, your income, your education, or any other human characteristic that we use to label or define ourselves.

And He is our Father who is "in heaven." Many of us have had loving earthly fathers, but many others of us have not. Many people have had fathers who have hurt or disappointed them, but our heavenly Father will never hurt us or disappoint us. He knows our every weakness and still loves us with a love that is beyond our understanding. He wants to hear the deepest longings of our hearts, and He wants to help us through life's journey.

"Hallowed be your name." *Hallowed* is another word for holy or consecrated or sacred. Jesus began by offering praise and worship to the one, true, almighty God. People in every generation have made gods of many things. But none of those gods are the true God like He is, and He has told us what His place in our lives should be. His commandment, "You shall have no other

gods before me" (Exodus 20:3), should cause us to evaluate our attitude toward Him as well as our schedules, our calendars, and our spending. Those things will tell us where He ranks among our priorities.

Because we recognize God's unique holiness, we will express our praise to Him. I don't mean just when you're at church, with music and singing filling the air. I mean that you should approach God with praise throughout the day. When you wake up in the morning, say, "God, You are holy and worthy of my worship. Thank You for all You will do in me and for me and through me today." When you arrive at your place of business, say, "God, thank You for my job. Help me to honor You here today." When you pull into your driveway after work, say, "God, thank You for my home and my family. Give us a good evening together. And bless my difficult neighbor across the street!" Before you drift off to sleep at night, say, "God, thank You for sustaining me through this day. Thank You for all the ways You have blessed me. I trust You with my life." When you let praise begin to resonate within you, soon it will begin to overflow so that everyone around you will see it!

"Your kingdom come, your will be done, on earth as it is in heaven." This is not a personal request; this is what intercession sounds like. "Father, let Your will break forth in me. Let Your will break forth in my home, in my church, in my neighborhood, in my nation." God has invested tremendous spiritual authority in you, and doors open when you pray. Conversely, doors stay closed when you don't. I believe that if you're willing to learn to become an intercessor, the Holy Spirit will teach you to pray more effectively and you will see outcomes that you had never imagined were possible.

"Give us today our daily bread." Jesus told us to pray for provision, and I think He meant provision for all of our needs. Note that He didn't ask for a pantry full of bread, but just enough for one day. This is tough for many of us. If you're like me, you'd like to have provisions for a lifetime all taken care of so you wouldn't have to think about that again. But that's not the attitude God wants us to have. He wants us to have faith in Him to provide. He expects us to work if we are able, of course, but He wants us to acknowledge that He is our Provider. And if we had a lifetime of provisions all wrapped up, we'd probably forget that and convince ourselves we'd done it all ourselves.

People are right to be cautious of what has come to be known as the prosperity gospel, but it's not presumptuous to express our needs to the Lord. Jesus has given you permission to ask God for everything you need—everything! He has promised to bless us abundantly, and we can count on Him to keep His promises. In turn, our responses should be humility and a grateful heart.

"And forgive us our debts, as we also have forgiven our debtors." Some versions use the word *trespasses* instead of *debts*, but both refer to sin, the debt we owe to God. Asking for forgiveness is a good habit to cultivate, and you might find it easier in the evening as things quiet down. As you look back over the day, you will be able to remember some things you didn't get quite right. Times when your words or actions did not honor the Lord. Words you said but shouldn't have. Words you should have said but didn't. Times you could've helped but didn't. Times when you put yourself ahead of others. And you will be able to forgive

anyone who has wronged or slighted you. It's good to end the day with a clean slate because Jesus said forgiveness or our lack of forgiveness has consequences: "For if you forgive other people when they sin against you, your heavenly Father will also forgive you. But if you do not forgive others their sins, your Father will not forgive your sins."

"And lead us not into temptation, but deliver us from the evil one." Jesus told us to actively pray that we would be protected from the temptation and testing of Satan. He had encountered many people who had succumbed to that lure and had even faced it Himself, so He had firsthand experience of its pull. Later, James reminded us, "When tempted, no one should say, 'God is tempting me.' For God cannot be tempted by evil, nor does he tempt anyone; but each person is tempted when they are dragged away by their own evil desire and enticed" (James 1:13–14). And Paul wanted the Corinthians to remember that "no temptation has overtaken you except what is common to mankind. And God is faithful; he will not let you be tempted beyond what you can bear. But when you are tempted, he will also provide a way out so that you can endure it" (1 Corinthians 10:13).

I find it comforting that when Jesus' disciples came to Him and said, "Please teach us to pray," He didn't laugh or turn away. He could have said, "Are you kidding? You guys are not very bright. Have you not been paying attention?" Instead, He was kind and generous. He said, "Sure, let Me help you with this. We'll start with something simple. Don't worry, you'll figure this out. And someday you'll be able to help other people."

THE HOLY SPIRIT, OUR HELPER

> In the same way, the Spirit helps us in our weakness. We do
> not know what we ought to pray for, but the Spirit himself
> intercedes for us through wordless groans. (Romans 8:26)

If you live in an area where multiple languages are commonly spoken, you may have seen a professional translator at work. The translator understands the languages of both people and can accurately communicate the thoughts of one to the other. Without a translator, communication in hospitals, government offices, and schools would be very difficult.

That's a good picture of the way the Holy Spirit helps us when we pray. There have been many times when I felt inadequate to express myself. Very often my pleas for help or healing or deliverance don't seem very organized or even coherent. And you might not believe this about a preacher, but sometimes I'm at a loss for words. I know that we all feel that way sometimes. It is an amazing promise that even when we don't know what to pray for or how to say it, the Holy Spirit is helping us by making the deepest longings of our hearts known to our Father.

THE POWER OF PERSISTENT PRAYER

> I rise before dawn and cry for help;
> I have put my hope in your word.
> My eyes stay open through the watches of the
>   night,

that I may meditate on your promises. (Psalm
119:147–148)

I could tell you many stories of the Lord honoring someone's
persistent prayers. I have seen hardened sinners saved, diseased
bodies healed, tenacious addictions defeated, broken families
restored, and more. But I want to tell you about a group of prayer
warriors who are living examples of faithfulness and persistence
in prayer.

Every morning from 6:30 to 7:30 a group of people meets at
our church to pray. It's an open group, and anyone is welcome to
come one day or every day. Some people pray silently, and others
pray aloud. The group began meeting in response to an invitation we had to go on a medical mission trip to a South American
country where there was a lot of political turmoil. My role would
be chief people mover, luggage handler, and box carrier. The plan
was to travel down the Amazon River at night and go ashore
before dawn. We would set up a clinic and then see medical and
dental patients from the surrounding jungle during the day. It's
a tropical region, with rains and high humidity and mosquitoes
so big they need a flight plan. Five separate vaccinations were
required just to enter the country. The real kicker for me was
when they told us we'd have to watch for snakes. It sounds like
an exciting adventure movie, but we were well aware of just how
challenging it would be.

A group of people who understood the power of prayer said
they would meet and pray every morning at 6:30 while we were
on that trip. One woman drove forty-five miles one way to be
a part of that group! As a result of their prayers, the trip went
really well. The temperature was milder than it should have been

in that season, and it didn't rain very much. The insects weren't a problem, and we didn't see any snakes. Most important, many lives were changed because we went—the lives of the people doing the praying and the lives of the people being prayed for.

And you know what? That group hasn't missed a day in over twenty years. No matter the weather or what else is going on in the world, they were there. The COVID-19 pandemic kept them from gathering in person for a while, but they adapted to video conferencing and met online until they could be together again. Today the open group meets Monday through Friday, and a core group of our church members meets on Saturday and Sunday.

This prayer ministry is not the most visible part of what we do, but it is an essential part of what we do. They have prayed people through desperate places, broken hearts, broken health, and broken families. They have prayed us through building projects, spiritual initiatives, events large and small, and all the other things that make up the life of an active and growing church. Their sheer determination to not stop praying inspires me, humbles me, and motivates me. And I credit much of the ministry success of our church to their persistent intercession.

If prayer is not a routine part of your life, you're missing something. I don't say that to burden you with guilt or shame. I say that to encourage you to begin imagining that putting time and effort into learning to interact with the God of the universe is worth the investment.

If you feel intimidated by the thought of consistent Bible reading and prayer, I encourage you to keep at it. Be persistent. Do not give up. Make the Holy Spirit welcome in your life and accept all the help He has to give. I used to think that everyone else had it all together and knew how to do all this "faith stuff" perfectly. From many years of living and listening and watching, I can assure you that is not true. We're all in this together, growing and learning as we keep showing up before Him, day after day.

PRAYER

Heavenly Father, grant me a revelation of Jesus, that I may know Him better and serve Him more fully. Thank You for the gift of Your Word and for its truth, its power, and its authority. Teach me to cherish its life-giving promises. Father, thank You for allowing me to come to You in prayer. Open my heart to hear Your voice. Show me how to depend on You to guide my steps so that the name of Jesus will be exalted through my life. In Jesus' name, amen.

CHAPTER 5

INSIDE INFORMATION (A BIBLICAL WORLDVIEW GIVES INSIGHT)

These things happened to them as examples and were written down as warnings for us, on whom the culmination of the ages has come.

—1 CORINTHIANS 10:11

Let's begin our discussion of the Bible and the worldview that springs from it by considering what the Bible is . . . and isn't. The Bible is simply God's written revelation to us. We also call it God's Word or Scripture, which means sacred writings. It consists of sixty-six books written by dozens of authors from varying cultural contexts over a long period of time. It contains many literary styles, including historical narratives, law codes, poems and songs, wise sayings, prophecies, firsthand accounts of Jesus' life and teachings, an account of the early days of the church, and letters.

> He determines the number of the stars
> and calls them each by name.
> Great is our Lord and mighty in power;
> his understanding has no limit. (Psalm 147:4–5)

The Bible is neither a history book nor a science book, and you will be frustrated if you try to make it into either one. However, I am absolutely convinced that God means what He says in His Word. When the Bible says that God knows how many stars are in the sky, and He has a name for every one of them, I believe it (Isaiah 40:26). When the Bible says that God knows how many hairs are on your head, I believe He has an accurate count after a few came out in your comb this morning (Matthew 10:30). I don't think Scripture is speaking about His knowledge in a poetic way; I believe God says what He means to say.

In an age of "smart" everything, I am baffled by our increasing willingness to depend on technology while we are increasingly reluctant to believe what God says. We allow unknown people and soulless technology to give us advice about which road to take and where to eat, but we question God's directives for navigating our journey through time. I'm not opposed to technology or science. In fact, I'm an advocate for both. But they cannot replace or exceed the knowledge of the God who created the heavens and the earth.

All Scripture is God-breathed and is useful for teaching, rebuking, correcting and training in righteousness, so that the servant of God may be thoroughly equipped for every good work. (2 Timothy 3:16–17)

I'm persuaded that the entirety of Scripture is inspired by God and that it is a necessary and profitable part of His provision for my life. And I believe all of it. There has never been a time when people were not reading the Scripture and picking and choosing what they thought was real, trustworthy, and relevant. But when Paul wrote to Timothy with advice about handling God's Word, he said "all" Scripture is from God. Enough said!

> **I'm persuaded that the entirety of Scripture is inspired by God and that it is a necessary and profitable part of His provision for my life.**

A BIBLICAL WORLDVIEW

The dictionary defines a worldview as "a comprehensive conception or apprehension of the world especially from a specific standpoint."[1] You may have heard someone say that they are operating from a philosophical worldview, or a scientific worldview, or a worldview based on a cultural perspective. Evangelical Christians look at the world through a biblical worldview. That simply means that we see the world through the lens of the Bible.

The unfortunate reality is that the difference between Christians and non-Christians is almost imperceptible today, because we're allowing the messaging that's driven by an ungodly worldview to fill our hearts and our minds and shape our dreams.

Researcher George Barna once commented, "If Jesus Christ came to this planet as a model of how we ought to live, then our goal should be to act like Jesus. Sadly, few people consistently demonstrate the love, obedience, and priorities of Jesus. The primary reason that people do not act like Jesus is because they do not think like Jesus." Barna went on to say, "Behavior stems from what we think—our attitudes, beliefs, values and opinions. Although most people own a Bible and know some of its content, our research found that most Americans have little idea how to integrate core biblical principles to form a unified and meaningful response to the challenges and opportunities of life. We're often more concerned with survival amidst chaos than with experiencing truth and significance."

The study went on to say that only 4 percent of the adults in a national survey had a biblical worldview at the heart of their decision-making. And it suggested that "a large share of the nation's moral and spiritual challenges is directly attributable to the absence of a biblical worldview among Americans."[2] This analysis, with its description of being "concerned with survival amidst chaos," sounds like it was written today, but it was published in 2003.

Another study, published in 2014, found that even among Christians, only 50 percent of evangelical Protestants believe "there are clear standards for what is right and wrong." Forty-eight percent said that "right or wrong depends on the situation." The remaining 2 percent were straddling the fence. In the same study, only 32 percent of mainline Protestants said there are clear standards of right and wrong.[3]

It's obvious that even Christians struggle with the place of

Scripture in our lives. I want to invite you to reflect on the place of God's Word in your own life and why you have assigned it that place. At the heart of the discussion is the question, "Can I trust the Word of God to speak to my life?" I hope that by the time we finish this chapter your answer will be a resounding "Yes!"

"WELL, THIS IS WHAT I THINK"

Some of the most frustrated people I meet are those who study the Bible endlessly but don't see the need to apply it personally. For them, reading Scripture is an academic exercise with the goal of picking it apart just as a biologist dissects an insect under a microscope.

Others have a challenge that we're reluctant to acknowledge: we approach our faith as if we're in a classroom setting where we do the assigned reading, hear a series of lectures, and then form our own opinions.

But the Bible is not an organism to be dissected or a theoretical, theological essay. The purpose of reading the Bible isn't to form an opinion about it or to agree or disagree with it. God gave us the Bible so that we can align our lives with it.

> God gave us the Bible so that we can align our lives with it.

We're entitled to believe whatever we want to believe because God has given us a free will. But God didn't give us the Bible to try to convince us that He is real or persuade us that He is worthy of our worship. He gave it to us so that we could choose to cooperate with Him in our generation.

There has been a push on the integrity of Scripture in recent years, but skepticism about the Bible is nothing new. The truth and relevance of the Scriptures have been questioned since the first day they were written down, but God does not need me to defend His integrity. The reality is that God's creation—including our physical bodies—will wither and fade, but God's Word will endure forever (Isaiah 40:6–8).

While discussion of the Bible will continue until the end of the age when Jesus returns, its purpose is really very simple. God intends for every generation to turn the Bible toward itself and act on what they see there. The wise and plainspoken James told us the folly of ignoring it and the blessing of heeding it:

> Do not merely listen to the word, and so deceive yourselves. Do what it says. Anyone who listens to the word but does not do what it says is like someone who looks at his face in a mirror and, after looking at himself, goes away and immediately forgets what he looks like. But whoever looks intently into the perfect law that gives freedom, and continues in it—not forgetting what they have heard, but doing it—they will be blessed in what they do. (James 1:22–25)

THE STORY OF THE BIBLE, FROM GENESIS TO REVELATION

Here is a simple description of the major events and themes of the Bible, beginning with Genesis and ending with Revelation.[4]

1. God spoke the universe into existence and brought order out of chaos. Life was perfect for a while, but it

didn't take long for humans to mess things up. God hit the reset button and wiped out everything and everyone with a flood—except for Noah, his family, and animals to repopulate the earth. Later, God's covenant with Abram began a story of redemption and blessing that has continued through the ages and is our spiritual heritage today.

2. God chose the Hebrew people for His own, but their story is not an easy one. The account of the exodus—of God using Moses to deliver His people out of generations of slavery—dramatically illustrates that God is actively involved in moving His people out of bondage and toward His purposes.

3. After Joshua fulfilled the assignment that Moses could not complete—leading God's people into the promised land—God raised up a series of judges. They were His voices to guide the children of Israel away from sin and toward repentance and blessing.

4. The Israelites wanted to be like the surrounding nations and have a king. God had Samuel warn them about the reality of life under an earthly king, but they persisted in their pleas. God allowed them to walk away from His best for them, and He asked Samuel to anoint a king. Samuel anointed first Saul and then David, whose son Solomon succeeded him on the throne.

5. After Solomon's death, the Israelites engaged in a civil war and divided into two nations—the Northern Kingdom (Israel) and the Southern Kingdom (Judah). In this period, known as the divided kingdom, the

people of Israel rebelled against the ways of God and experienced serious consequences.

6. God appointed messengers called prophets to represent Himself to His people. They brought words of both chastisement and hope. Their messages, while sometimes difficult to understand and unpopular, remind us that God does not stand removed from history but is concerned with the lives of His people.

7. God warned His people again and again that their unfaithfulness would have dire consequences, and He eventually allowed them to be conquered and driven into exile. Their suffering was crushing, but in the midst of it came some of the greatest demonstrations of God's presence and power.

8. The books of Job, Psalms, Proverbs, Ecclesiastes, and the Song of Solomon are called the Wisdom Literature. These books do not fit neatly into a timeline. They offer God's wisdom for facing the challenges of life, reminders of God's faithfulness, and the certainty that God is watching over all things.

9. When Nehemiah heard that the Israelites returning to Jerusalem from exile had rebuilt God's temple but the city was in shambles, he was eager to rebuild the wall and shore up the city's defenses. He accepted this assignment from God, then organized the people and completed the wall even in the face of ridicule and hostility.

10. Jesus' life and ministry are an exact representation of the character of God and the reality that the patterns of ministry we see in the Old Testament foreshadowed. The Gospels are not the beginning of a new

story but the fulfillment of the story that began in Genesis. They help us understand Jesus as the Christ, the Messiah of prophecy. The narrative of Scripture pivoted when the sinless, perfect, obedient Son of God received all the punishment that was due to us for our wickedness and rebellion so that we in turn might receive all the blessings that were due to Him for His perfect obedience. Jesus is the turning point of history—with Him, everything changed.

11. A few weeks after Jesus' ascension to heaven, thousands of people in Jerusalem heard and believed His message preached by the disciples and received the Holy Spirit. This Jerusalem awakening spread to the surrounding area, and many believed, even in the midst of great persecution against followers of Jesus.

12. In Acts 9–10 we are reminded that Jesus is the head of the church and that the church is the expression of God's love and truth to the world. Saul was recruited to the cause of Christ and became the apostle Paul. A seismic shift in the direction of the church occurred when Peter was shown that the Jesus-story is not just for the Jewish people, but for everyone.

13. The Roman world heard the Jesus-story as His followers were persecuted and scattered. Paul and the other apostles faced great trials as they traveled from city to city, yet the church gained momentum as they pressed on and faithfully shared the message. Many came to faith during this time.

14. In spite of the many hardships Paul faced during his years of ministry, he remained an unrelenting advocate

for Jesus. Following Jesus is still about accepting His invitation to offer yourself as a living sacrifice and become an ambassador for the kingdom of God.

15. The book of Revelation is a story of tremendous hope. It describes the triumphant return of our Lord to defeat His enemies and deliver His people from this current evil age. The messages of Revelation—The King is coming! Trust in God! Overcome!—are so important that John, Jesus' friend and most trusted disciple, was chosen to be the recipient and the bearer of this good news.

We'll all admit that parts of the Bible can be difficult to read and hard to understand. And we'll never feel confident pronouncing all those Old Testament names! But the objective of the Bible is clear: from Genesis to Revelation, God is showing us that we need to have a relationship with Him and is pointing us to His Son, Jesus, as the only way that is possible. And God's motive? Love. Absolute, unimaginable love.

A WORD ABOUT CREATION

In the beginning God created the heavens and the earth. (Genesis 1:1)

The Bible opens with the presentation of God as the Creator and Sustainer and begins the account of His relationship with Adam and his descendants. It is difficult to overestimate the significance of accepting God as the Creator. In our arrogance, we've attempted to set the notion aside. If you'll accept this statement as true, that God did indeed create our world, then the rest of the Bible will open up for you and make sense.

On the other hand, if you reject God as Creator, the rest of the Bible will be nonsense. Why would you believe that God cares about us? Why would you believe that God would send His Son to the earth to be born of a virgin? Why would you believe that Jesus performed miracles and that He Himself rose from the dead? Why would you believe that there is a heaven and trust God for an eternity with Him there?

The Bible is not a textbook of theoretical physics, nor is it the complete story of everything God has ever done. When the narrative begins, the earth already exists but in a chaotic state—and Genesis describes how God brought order out of the chaos. But it is not a coincidence that we are presented with this important principle in its opening words.

If you've pushed aside the notion of God as Creator, I want you to invite it back into your awareness. Simply acknowledge that this world and everything in it came from God and that each of us is more than a random mass of cells brought together by chance. We are unique creations of an all-knowing God, and the world and everything in it are a testimony to His goodness. This is a firm foundation for a life of faith.

AN OPEN-BOOK TEST

He has shown you, O mortal, what is good.
And what does the LORD require of you?

To act justly and to love mercy
and to walk humbly with your God. (Micah
6:8)

What are some of the sweetest words for a student facing an exam? "This will be an open-book test." You have listened to lectures, read the assigned material, done your homework, and prepared for the test. Then you arrive in class and hear that message—hallelujah!

Did you know that the Christian life is an open-book test? We have been given God's textbook. We have been told what God requires of us. And we have been provided with the patient yet persistent tutoring of the Holy Spirit. There are no favorites in God's classroom, and there are no secret lectures provided to only a few. We all have been given the same information about what He expects: to act justly, to love mercy, and to walk humbly with God. So let's open the book!

IT BEGAN WITH STONE TABLETS

Remember the Ten Commandments? We get them really early in the story, in Exodus 20:3–17. God's people were newly freed from generations of slavery, and they needed guidelines for how to live—with Him and with each other. The commandments are not suggestions or recommendations; they are ten statements given directly by God, and they have never been amended or rescinded. God did not obscure His rules in the rhymes of poetry or the mysticism of prophecy. They are self-explanatory and simple enough for all to understand. Let's look at these instructions that God gave to Moses.

1. You shall have no other gods before me.
2. You shall not make for yourself an image in the form of anything in heaven above or on the earth beneath or in the waters below. You shall not bow down to them or worship them; for I, the LORD your God, am a jealous God, punishing the children for the sin of the parents to the third and fourth generation of those who hate me, but showing love to a thousand generations of those who love me and keep my commandments.
3. You shall not misuse the name of the LORD your God, for the LORD will not hold anyone guiltless who misuses his name.
4. Remember the Sabbath day by keeping it holy. Six days you shall labor and do all your work, but the seventh day is a sabbath to the LORD your God. On it you shall not do any work, neither you, nor your son or daughter, nor your male or female servant, nor your animals, nor any foreigner residing in your towns. For in six days the LORD made the heavens and the earth, the sea, and all that is in them, but he rested on the seventh day. Therefore the LORD blessed the Sabbath day and made it holy.
5. Honor your father and your mother, so that you may live long in the land the LORD your God is giving you.
6. You shall not murder.

7. You shall not commit adultery.
8. You shall not steal.
9. You shall not give false testimony against your neighbor.
10. You shall not covet your neighbor's house. You shall not covet your neighbor's wife, or his male or female servant, his ox or donkey, or anything that belongs to your neighbor.

AT THE HEART OF OUR NATION

The Ten Commandments were at the heart of America's founding and were revered and abided by for many generations. They were publicly displayed in schools, courthouses, and other government buildings, and many people could say them from memory. In 1980, the ruling in *Stone v. Graham* outlawed the display of the Ten Commandments in our public schools. The court chose to ignore the fact that the Decalogue was the fundamental legal code of Western civilization and the basis of common law in America. "Freedom of religion" has been confused with "freedom from religion" as the Establishment Clause has emerged to dominate this discussion. Sweeping aside generations of practice when the Bible and prayer were welcome in public discourse, the Supreme Court said, "If the posted copies of the Ten Commandments are to have any effect at all, it will be to induce the schoolchildren to read, meditate upon, perhaps to venerate and obey, the Commandments. However desirable this might be as a matter of private devotion, it is not a permissible state objective under the Establishment Clause."[5]

That precedent had far-reaching ramifications, and the Ten Commandments have been removed from many public displays. This cannot be blamed on the ungodly. This has happened on our watch. We haven't stood our posts as watchmen on the walls. We've allowed the Ten Commandments to be removed, and we've watched as they've been replaced by law enforcement officers and metal detectors. Can we not see the connection?

In our nation's history, Christians have been at the forefront of the fight for freedom and tolerance. Equal rights for women, children, minorities, and the powerless did not arise on their own. We assume these freedoms are shared around the world; I assure you they are not. Judeo-Christian values based on the Ten Commandments have provided that framework in the United States for over two hundred years, and that is what separates us from many cultures of the world.

I will be the first to admit that our nation is not perfect. But if we neglect or set aside the values that established our freedoms, our freedoms will fade and disappear. It's important to note that it is not unique to this generation for people to say, "I don't want you to say that God had anything to do with the founding of our country." However, this is our watch, and I intend to do everything in my power to remind our culture that the founding of our nation was based on principles that honor God. I hope you will join me.

THOSE WISE AND WITTY PROVERBS

At first glance the book of Proverbs may just look like a collection of wise and sometimes witty sayings. But it's more than the musings of one man or even the collected wisdom of the Jewish people. The Proverbs are a response from God to Solomon's request for wisdom. God was so pleased by Solomon's humble request that he supernaturally inspired him with wisdom and insight greater than any who had come before or who would come after (1 Kings 3:9–12).

So when we read the book of Proverbs, we are not just reading the good ideas of a smart person; we are reaping the benefits of what God poured into Solomon's life. The book of Proverbs gives us a clear window into the hearts and motives of people. It tells us what will happen if we choose A or B, and then we can make an informed choice. Let's look at some of Solomon's sayings.

> Above all else, guard your heart,
> for everything you do flows from it. (4:23)

We put a lot of effort into protecting ourselves from various things. We wear sunscreen and lock our houses. We protect our personal data and our investments. All those things are good and necessary, but Solomon said we should give even more attention to guarding our hearts—"Above all else," actually. Why? Because what happens *to* us is a small matter compared to what happens *within* us. And he knew that everything in our lives flows from our inward state—the condition of our hearts.

We guard our hearts intentionally by doing things such as seeking understanding of the Lord and His purposes for us; using discernment when choosing friends; and being a Spirit-filled consumer of television, movies, and music. The condition of your heart will determine the course of your life both in time and eternity, so follow Solomon's advice and guard it with great care.

Can a man scoop fire into his lap
without his clothes being burned?
Can a man walk on hot coals without his feet
being scorched?
So is he who sleeps with another man's wife;
no one who touches her will go unpunished.
(6:27–29)

God often gives us insight into the ending of something at the beginning. Here Solomon told us the destructive results of adultery. Elsewhere in Proverbs we read that adultery leads to financial ruin and even death. That is why the Bible warns us against any sexual activity outside marriage. God loves us, so He warns us that the fire of temptation will lead to extreme discomfort.

Adultery is just one issue we are warned about. I believe in the power of God's forgiveness and the sufficiency of the blood of Jesus to wash away sin and redeem lives. But those things don't change the counsel of Scripture. If we as Christ followers ignore the warning lights and drive onto the train tracks, we shouldn't be surprised when the train hits us. God is not being mean-spirited; it's simply that He wants us to be aware that there will be consequences for sinful behavior and we should heed His boundaries.

A cheerful heart is good medicine,
but a crushed spirit dries up the bones. (17:22)

You may have heard it said that every person brings joy—some when they arrive, and others when they leave! We have emotional visitors as well: those you are glad to see coming, and those you are glad to see going. Disappointment and discouragement are two of those visitors who show up uninvited from time to time. Some of us have let them linger for so long that they seem like old friends, but they are not our friends. They are soul-crushing adversaries, and we should not welcome them. Nor should we wait around and hope that they will eventually find their way to the door; we should take the initiative and kick them out.

Solomon knew that a cheerful heart is contagious, so instead of dwelling on disappointment and discouragement, let's find positive people who are willing to walk alongside us and encourage us. Let's focus on the blessings and provision God has shown us. Let's be grateful for our freedom to worship, to serve together, to lift up the name of Jesus in our homes and communities. Let's be cheerful. Let's choose joy!

> By wisdom a house is built,
> and through understanding it is established;
> through knowledge its rooms are filled
> with rare and beautiful treasures. (24:3–4)

The devil is evil, and he does not play fair. He exploits us when we are emotionally undeveloped and not prepared to push back against him. That's why honoring God in our homes and creating houses filled with spiritual treasures is so critical. We are a spiritual line of defense for the young people who live in our homes as well as all the other children who live in our society. That's why we stand for God's definition of marriage and family. That's why we promote Christian foster homes and adoptive families. That's why we stand for godliness in the public schools. That's why we promote God's standards in the world of entertainment.

God's wisdom, understanding, and knowledge combine to create a Christian worldview that protects the most vulnerable among us, especially those who don't yet have the maturity to defend themselves. Solomon knew that it would take godly wisdom, understanding, and knowledge to build a spiritually strong household.

"IF" AND "THEREFORE"

One of the things I love about the Bible is that it tells us the outcomes of so many choices. Jesus' lengthy Sermon on the Mount (Matthew 5–7) is a great example. He tells us not to judge others so that we won't be judged. He says if you choose meekness, you will inherit the earth—what a promise! And if you choose purity, you will see God—what a blessing! The Bible does not give a specific answer to every one of life's questions, but it certainly gives guidance that will help us make decisions. Here's one of Jesus' "if" statements.

> And when you stand praying, if you hold anything against anyone, forgive them, so that your Father in heaven may forgive you your sins. (Mark 11:25)

"If you hold anything against anyone." Did you know that God's forgiveness is conditional? You have to meet His condition in order to receive His forgiveness, and the condition is that we have to be willing to forgive others—anyone for anything.

Preachers are famous for eliciting rolling eyes and audible groans when they say, "When you see 'therefore' in the Bible, you need to ask what it's there for!" Let's look at one of those "therefore" statements.

> Therefore, I urge you, brothers and sisters, in view of God's mercy, to offer your bodies as a living sacrifice, holy and pleasing to God—this is your true and proper worship. (Romans 12:1)

The book of Romans is a masterful yet simple presentation of theology. In the first eleven chapters, Paul described the downward progression of human character when we reject God and choose sin. He went into great detail about the righteousness that God requires and how it is available to us only through Jesus' sacrificial death and glorious resurrection. Then comes the convicting opening of chapter 12: "Therefore, because of God's great mercy toward you, I beg you to offer yourself as a living sacrifice to Him!" Paul's "therefore" invitation speaks just as loudly to us as it did to those Roman Christians. Because of all God has done for us, we should naturally want to serve and honor Him.

"I AM"

> Moses said to God, "Suppose I go to the Israelites and say to them, 'The God of your fathers has sent me to you,' and they ask me, 'What is his name?' Then what shall I tell them?"
> God said to Moses, "I AM WHO I AM. This is what you are to say to the Israelites: 'I AM has sent me to you.'"
> (Exodus 3:13–14)

"I AM" is the profoundly simple yet awe-inspiring name that God told Moses to tell the Israelites in the likely event that they questioned his authority to lead them. Jesus also made seven well-known "I am" statements that describe His role in the unfolding story of God's interaction with people:

> Then Jesus declared, "I am the bread of life. Whoever comes to me will never go hungry, and whoever believes in me will never be thirsty." (John 6:35)

Jesus is certainly concerned about our physical hunger, but He is even more concerned about our spiritual hunger.

> When Jesus spoke again to the people, he said, "I am the light of the world. Whoever follows me will never walk in darkness, but will have the light of life." (John 8:12)

Jesus did not say He is "a light in the world." He said He is "the light of the world." Jesus is the only light capable of piercing through the evil we face, and He is our only hope of protection against evil.

> Therefore Jesus said again, "Very truly I tell you, I am the gate for the sheep. All who have come before me are thieves and robbers, but the sheep have not listened to them. I am the gate; whoever enters through me will be saved. They will come in and go out, and find pasture." (John 10:7–9)

Jesus described Himself as the only pathway to God and the

only haven of safety in the world. All false teachers are thieves and robbers.

> "I am the good shepherd. The good shepherd lays down his life for the sheep . . . I am the good shepherd; I know my sheep and my sheep know me." (John 10:11, 14)

Jesus is the only shepherd who is truly good and the only one willing to give up His life for His sheep.

> Jesus said to her, "I am the resurrection and the life. The one who believes in me will live, even though they die; and whoever lives by believing in me will never die." (John 11:25–26)

Only Jesus can do more than talk about resurrection and life. Jesus *is* the resurrection and life, and He alone can offer us the gift of eternal life.

> Jesus answered, "I am the way and the truth and the life. No one comes to the Father except through me." (John 14:6)

Jesus didn't say that He would show us the way, or tell us the truth, or instruct us about life. He said He *is* those things, and the only way to the Father.

> "I am the true vine, and my Father is the gardener. . . . I am the vine; you are the branches." (John 15:1, 5)

The image of a grapevine would have been very familiar to

Jesus' listeners. He is the true vine, and we are His branches. We will live and bear fruit only if we are firmly joined to Him.

A TEXT WITHOUT A CONTEXT
IS A PRETEXT

Skeptics will say that you can prove anything you want to with your Bible if you rip a verse out of its context and paste it together with something else. And they are correct. While that is true, and while understanding the context of a verse is important, there's another way of understanding Scripture. That's when a verse from the Word of God becomes a reality in your life, and your life becomes the context for that passage. That gives it a significance beyond the historical context and makes it real in you.

For example, Romans 10:9 says, "If you declare with your mouth, 'Jesus is Lord,' and believe in your heart that God raised him from the dead, you will be saved." You can identify its context as part of Paul's message to the believers in Rome. You can understand the larger discussion of the redemptive work of Christ and His substitutionary death on our behalf. You can approach all of those things from a theological perspective and be absolutely correct. Or you can evaluate it from a literary standpoint and discuss the writing style, and Paul's use of certain words, and where it falls in the story of the Bible. That, too, would be correct.

But when that verse finds a context in your life, and you declare those things about Jesus with your mouth and believe them in your heart, it takes on an entirely different meaning in you and transforms your life. The Bible was never intended to be studied as a history book, or a science book, or a philosophy book; it was intended to address our lives. It was given to us that we might know the nature of God and that we might live in such a way that we can spend eternity in His presence.

SO WHAT NOW?

> I seek you with all my heart;
> do not let me stray from your commands.
> I have hidden your word in my heart
> that I might not sin against you. (Psalm
>   119:10–11)

The best way to understand the Bible is simple: start reading it. I think the wisest, most contented people I know are the ones who spend consistent time in God's Word. I have read the Bible from cover to cover several times, and it seems like I get something new from it every time I open the book. I read from different translations, and the words may sound a little different, but it is more than that.

I have changed since I last read through the Bible. I am in a different season of life. The world around me is changing. The challenges I face are changing. But God's truth for us never changes. It is there to guide us, motivate us, refresh us, and reassure us. It is there to give us a biblical worldview. Open God's Word and allow it to speak to you, and He will show you something new every day.

SOME THINGS TO THINK ABOUT

1. Which do you place more trust in—your smartphone or the Word of God?

2. Belief in God as the Creator is the first step of faith. Do you have a settled conviction that God created the world and everything in it? Do you believe that He will sustain it according to His plans and purposes?

3. Do you honor the Ten Commandments in your life and in your home? Are you filling your home with spiritual treasures?

4. Do you spend as much effort guarding your heart as you do protecting your possessions? Does the Holy Spirit control your consumption of music and entertainment?

5. Have you allowed disappointment and discouragement to take up residence in your heart? If so, how can you see them through a proper spiritual perspective and make a conscious decision to choose joy?

6. Do you study the Bible as a scientist attempting to pick it apart or as a follower of Jesus seeking a transformed life?

7. Is your Bible a vital and necessary part of your daily routine? Do you have God's Word in your heart so that you can lean on it in times of trouble?

CHAPTER 6

KNOW THE RIGHT PEOPLE

When they saw the courage of Peter and John and realized that
they were unschooled, ordinary men, they were astonished and
they took note that these men had been with Jesus.
—ACTS 4:13

I t's not what you know. It's who you know."

We often say that in a disparaging way, but there is truth
in that old saying. If you are physically sick, it helps if you know a
trained and trustworthy doctor. And if you are looking for a job,
a reliable and supportive network certainly helps. On the other
hand, if you put your trust in people who are not able to provide the proper assistance, you're making yourself vulnerable.
If you know people with ability and capability, they can help

you address the circumstances you're facing. It's a tremendous advantage.

The reality of our world is that trouble is here and more trouble is coming. None of us will be able to successfully navigate the coming days alone. You need to know reliable, trustworthy people who can help you today and also help you secure your future.

The benefits of an earthly support network are real, but they pale in comparison to the benefits that come to us when we learn to depend on God. No earthly family, no group of friends, no mentor or paid professional knows you as intimately and cares about you as deeply as God does. Our God is the almighty Creator of the universe and everything in it, including you. He knows your strengths and weaknesses. He knows your thoughts. He knows what you are going to say before you say it and what you are going to do before you do it. And He is no impartial observer, but your Creator who looks at you with eyes of love and compassion.

I want you to believe in the possibilities of God. That's easy to say, but it can be hard to live out. We've been trained to equate our relationship with God with performing certain behaviors. We know how to dress and talk like Christians. We know how to show up at church, stand and sit at the right times, sing along with the group, and drop something in the offering plate. Some of us have been taking Christian acting lessons since childhood, and we play that role very well.

It is not easy to break away from that. It is not a comfortable process to exchange those outward expressions of religion for the sweeping imagination of what God is capable of doing in us and through us. But our God is mighty, powerful, and bigger than a to-do list that we check off week after week. Just how big is our God? Let's stretch ourselves a little and examine the character and attributes of the God of the Bible.

THE GOD OF THE BIBLE: THREE IN ONE

Many volumes have been written about what is known as the Trinity, or the three-in-one personhood of God. While the term *Trinity* is never used in the Bible, we know the concept is important because it is introduced in the first verses of Scripture:

> In the beginning God created the heavens and the earth. Now the earth was formless and empty, darkness was over the surface of the deep, and the Spirit of God was hovering over the waters. (Genesis 1:1–2)

It is not apparent in English, but two of these words that we read as singular are plural in Hebrew—"God" in verse 1 and "Spirit of God" in verse 2. Later, John confirmed that Jesus, "the Word," was present from the beginning and active in creation: "In the beginning was the Word, and the Word was with God, and the Word was God. He was with God in the beginning. Through him all things were made; without him nothing was made that has been made" (John 1:1–3).

The Trinity is unexplainable in human terms, but water offers us a helpful analogy. Water exists in three forms, and each has benefits for us: as a liquid that we drink; as a solid, ice, that we use to cool our drinks; and as a vapor, steam, that we use to take wrinkles out of our clothes. Whether it's a liquid or a solid or a vapor, the chemical formula is the same: H_2O. It may look different and achieve different purposes for us, but its substance never changes. The three members of the Trinity are different, yet each is fully God. If we fail to pursue a relationship with any of the three, we will forfeit part of how God wants to interact with us and help us.

The notion of a triune God is woven throughout the Bible: three divine persons in one essence—God the Father, God the Son, and God the Holy Spirit. We see all three members of the Trinity at work throughout Scripture. We see God the Father loving us, pursuing us, and desiring to redeem us from the consequences of our sinful natures. We see God the Son coming to earth to live and die, fully God and fully man, able to both save us and relate to us as a brother. We see God the Spirit empowering us, revealing spiritual things to us, and helping us navigate life's challenges, interceding for us with the Father.

I can't fully explain the complexity of the Trinity, but I've come to terms with that. I have simply placed my trust in God that He is who He is.

God Sent His Son

> But when the set time had fully come, God sent his Son, born of a woman, born under the law, to redeem those under the law, that we might receive adoption to sonship. (Galatians 4:4–5)

Jesus arrived in Bethlehem because of a God initiative. He laid aside the privilege of heaven and humbled Himself to become a part of His creation. He became obedient to His Father's will, accepting an assignment that would lead to a Roman cross, a brutal death, and a world-changing resurrection.

Some people say that the timing of Jesus' birth was related to the way Roman civilization had created opportunities for the spread of the gospel. That is true, because the Romans were organized go-getters who were purposeful about expanding their territory. Around 300 BC they had begun building a network of roads that made it easier to transport people, goods, and their military across their expanding empire. Their language, Latin, was spoken over much of their known world, and they adopted many ideas from Greek culture as well. It was the first time in human history that an idea could be communicated across a broad area with relative ease.

But the timing of Jesus' coming was based on more than convenient transportation and communication. For hundreds of years God had patiently given His people a series of judges, kings, and prophets, but they had fallen into corruption and disarray in spite of His help. The Romans were more than happy to step into the power vacuum created by the turmoil in Jerusalem.

When we get to the New Testament, we're fifty years into Roman rule. The temple was still standing prominently in Jerusalem, the daily sacrifices were still taking place, and the three pilgrimage festivals were still celebrated every year. But the Jewish people had become weary of their overlords, and they were looking for a Messiah with increasing desperation. However, they weren't interested in the Suffering Servant that Isaiah had prophesied about five hundred years before (Isaiah 53); they wanted a military conqueror and deliverer who would throw out the pagan Romans and reestablish their autonomy and liberty.

Jesus revealed Himself and began His ministry in the midst

of this hotbed of political, cultural, and religious unrest. John the Baptist had been telling people that the Messiah was coming and calling people to repent—not by performing their usual ritual bathing in one of the pools surrounding the temple but by walking twenty miles into the desert to be baptized in a river by a man who let his hair grow long, wore a garment of camel's hair, and ate a diet of locusts and wild honey (Matthew 3).

So many people were responding to this unusual man that the religious leaders in Jerusalem were compelled to travel out to the Jordan River to see what he was up to. All of these things happening at the same time meant the atmosphere within Judaism and the broader world was ripe for the coming of the Messiah— and so God's Son, Jesus of Nazareth, made Himself known.

Jesus Changed Everything

> If you declare with your mouth, "Jesus is Lord," and believe in your heart that God raised him from the dead, you will be saved. (Romans 10:9)

Many years ago I studied at Hebrew University in Jerusalem. One class that I remember vividly was on the Jewish background of Christianity. The professor was a young Orthodox Jewish scholar, probably no older than I was at the time, and he was brilliant. We could write our papers in any one of seven languages—I chose English! I can still picture his hands; they were red and chapped from the ritual washing he performed throughout the day.

The only time I saw him uncomfortable was in two sessions when he taught about the death and resurrection of Jesus. He finally stopped and said, "Those people in the first century, they really believed that Jesus was raised from the dead." Then he hung his head for a moment and said, "If I believed that, I'd have to be a Christian too."

The decision of those first disciples to follow Jesus was a huge step of faith, but it was a step that would completely transform their lives. Most of those men were just regular, blue-collar guys. But when they followed Jesus, their lives were changed. Whereas once they were virtually unknown to all but their immediate circle, now they have been celebrated around the earth for centuries and continue to make an impact for God. I won't promise you that following Jesus will make your name known throughout the world, but it will give you opportunities to serve Him in ways that will bless you and others for eternity.

Jesus showed person after person that their family backgrounds didn't matter, their conditions were not permanent, and their sins were not too terrible to be forgiven. He gave Peter a life-changing demonstration of how radical faith can keep you afloat when conventional wisdom says you should be sinking. And He showed Paul that anyone's life can make a U-turn and become productive for His kingdom.

So whatever your life's calling, or whoever your circle of friends is, let it be known that you're an advocate for Jesus. If the truth about Jesus is going to spread, it will be a grassroots initiative where you and I are unrelenting advocates for Him.

> Let it be known that you're an advocate for Jesus.

We must not be silent; we must tell the God-story that we have to tell. In all of your brokenness, in all of your weakness, and in all that you are not, keep on talking about Jesus. Don't stop, no matter what obstacles or opposition you face.

If you haven't been willing to do that, take a moment right now to tell the Lord you're sorry. A day is coming when you're going to meet Jesus face-to-face. And when that moment arrives, you want Him to greet you with a smile and welcome you as a loyal friend.

God Sent His Spirit

> [Jesus said,] "And I will ask the Father, and he will give you another advocate to help you and be with you forever—the Spirit of truth." (John 14:16–17)

The arrival of the Holy Spirit to help God's people was just as much God directed as Jesus' incarnation. We could not save ourselves apart from Jesus' redemptive work. We cannot fulfill God's purposes for our lives without the help of the Spirit of God.

Jesus and the Holy Spirit are the two greatest gifts that God has ever given to humanity. Both Jesus and the Holy Spirit are God, and they express His power for our deliverance and well-being. We need to have a relationship with both of them.

An Exchange of Persons—"I'm going away"

Let's backtrack a little. For a while, Jesus had been trying to prepare the disciples for what was coming—an exchange of two divine persons—but they never really understood what He meant. In the disciples' defense, it was something they had no capacity to imagine. And I don't think we have any framework for imagining the roller coaster ride of emotions they experienced during those few weeks.

Jesus told them that He would be leaving, but that was not the bargain they had struck. "Follow Me, and I'll make you fishers of men," He had said. And for three years they had followed Him up into the hills and down into the valleys. They had gone with Him into the crowds and into the lonely places. They had experienced unimaginable things and expanded their understanding of God.

When Jesus and His disciples were in Jerusalem to celebrate the Passover, it probably seemed that they were on the path to achieving all they had sacrificed for and worked toward. There was growing enthusiasm for Jesus' message, and He had been met by happy crowds waving palm branches.

But privately Jesus was saying, "I'm going away. And where I'm going, you can't come." I'm sure the disciples were stunned. "What? We left everything behind to follow You. Just tell us where You're going, and we'll come too. It doesn't matter where, we want to go." He would not relent, but insisted, "No, you can't come. But I'm going to send a Helper for you." "A helper?" they must have whispered among themselves. "We don't need a helper! Jesus is the One who feeds the crowds and raises the dead and casts out demons! We need Him!"

The situation went downhill fast over the next few days. Judas betrayed Jesus after their Passover meal. Jesus was arrested. Peter denied Him publicly—three times. Jesus endured a sham trial and was quickly executed. Three days later His tomb was discovered empty. Then the Jesus they had last seen hanging dead on a cross appeared to them very much alive, with scars to prove His identity and His torturous ordeal.

Can you imagine what they must have felt when Jesus told

them that He was leaving them yet again? Anger? Confusion? Fear? Despair? Even when He said, "It is to your advantage that I go away," I imagine they were thinking, *No, it's not!*

We can sympathize with their very human emotions. But in the rearview mirror of history, we can see that this was God's plan from the beginning. Just as the disciples benefited from Jesus' days on the earth, so do we. And just as the disciples benefited from the coming of the Holy Spirit, so do we.

What Does the Holy Spirit Do?

The Holy Spirit is our personal spiritual trainer. "I have many more things to say to you, but you cannot bear them at the present time. But when He, the Spirit of truth, comes, He will guide you into all the truth; for He will not speak on His own, but whatever He hears, He will speak; and He will disclose to you what is to come" (John 16:12–13 NASB).

> The redemptive work of Jesus is finished, but our training in righteousness is far from complete.

Jesus realized the disciples had much to learn, and He was leaving. God's resolution to the dilemma was the person of the Holy Spirit, the abiding presence of God within His people. God's Spirit would no longer dwell in the tabernacle or the temple but within each of His people. After Jesus completed His redemptive work and left the earth to return to heaven, the Father sent the Holy Spirit. God's Spirit remains with us and offers yet another kind of revelation and help. The redemptive work of Jesus is finished, but our training in righteousness is far from complete. The Father had faith that the Son would do His job. And it's very clear from Scripture that Jesus had complete trust that the Holy Spirit would carry on what He had begun.

The Holy Spirit dwells in the church, the body of Christ. "In him the whole building is joined together and rises to become a holy temple in the Lord. And in him you too are being built together to become a dwelling in which God lives by his Spirit" (Ephesians 2:21–22). The Holy Spirit is the administrator of everything that belongs to Jesus, and that includes the church. Jesus is Lord *of* the church, but the Holy Spirit is Lord *in* the church. The church of Jesus Christ is not a building, or a denomination, but every person who has acknowledged Jesus of Nazareth as the Messiah, accepted Him as Lord, and serves Him as King. We're more than a group of individuals scattered around the globe. We are a body, a unified whole, and the Holy Spirit is working to help us grow to maturity, individually, and collectively.

The Holy Spirit empowers the body of Christ to share the gospel. "But you will receive power when the Holy Spirit comes on you; and you will be my witnesses in Jerusalem, and in all Judea and Samaria, and to the ends of the earth" (Acts 1:8). After the Holy Spirit's arrival, the disciples became an unstoppable force. Their witness started in Jerusalem, then expanded to Judea, and then Samaria. If you chart that on a map, you see that those are expanding concentric circles like ripples on a pond after a stone has been dropped. And "the ends of the earth" includes us!

After the Holy Spirit came on the Day of Pentecost in Acts 2, the entire city was stirred. The people who had shouted, "Crucify Him!" a few days earlier were now asking, "What must we do to be saved?" Within a matter of months, the surrounding communities were experiencing the same thing. The Holy Spirit has empowered the church to be His witnesses in the world throughout the generations, and that includes us today.

The Holy Spirit intercedes for us with the Father. "In the same way, the Spirit helps us in our weakness. We do not know what we ought to pray for, but the Spirit himself intercedes for us through wordless groans" (Romans 8:26). We each have burdens that sometimes threaten to overwhelm us. Job loss, financial setbacks, prodigal children, illness, separation and divorce, depression, addictions, pressures at school and at work—the list goes on. I often begin to pray but find myself unable to adequately express my deepest emotions, longings, and burdens. I imagine you have experienced the same thing. It is a great relief to know that the Holy Spirit is always present, listening and interceding for us even when we don't know how we should pray.

The Holy Spirit convicts us of sin and invites us toward godliness. "And we all, who with unveiled faces contemplate the Lord's glory, are being transformed into his image with ever-increasing glory, which comes from the Lord, who is the Spirit" (2 Corinthians 3:18). The Holy Spirit shines His light into our lives and makes us aware of things that are limiting what we could be for the Lord. It could be a thought pattern, an attitude, a habit, or a whole host of things that we need to address.

I am amused when people say to me, "This Christian stuff must be easier for you because you're a preacher." I don't usually start naming all of my weaknesses, but you can rest assured that I have them and that I am struggling toward spiritual maturity with everyone else. If we are truly going to be transformed, we will have to welcome a power greater than ourselves. We won't study our Bibles or even pray our way into transformation. We yield to the Spirit of God, who transforms us.

ALL THINGS ARE POSSIBLE

> Jesus looked at them and said, "With man this is impossible, but not with God; all things are possible with God." (Mark 10:27)

Throughout Scripture, both the Old Testament and the New Testament, the presence of God's Spirit is synonymous with His power. And it isn't just visible demonstrations of power. It's about the revelation and understanding of God, the insight and wisdom of God. I'm an advocate for learning, and education, and training, and discipline. They're all very important things. But we need resources beyond our own intellect and understanding and life experience. That's where the Spirit of God helps us. He brings us insight, discernment, wisdom, and knowledge that we would never be able to attain on our own. If we are going to navigate life's journey successfully, we must open our hearts to all He has to offer us.

God is not defined or confined by our limited expectations.

We have some rather fixed ideas of what God can do, should do, and will do. But Scripture is full of accounts of God showing that He is not defined or confined by our limited expectations.

The Spirit of the LORD came powerfully upon him. The ropes on his arms became like charred flax, and the bindings dropped from his hands. Finding a fresh jawbone of a donkey, he grabbed it and struck down a thousand men. (Judges 15:14–15)

Samson is the strong man of the Bible. When the Spirit of the Lord came upon him, he could perform remarkable physical feats. Scripture says that Samson's Philistine enemies couldn't figure out why he was so strong, so I don't think he looked like a pumped-up gym rat. I think Samson looked like a regular guy, and the Spirit of God gave him supernatural strength in order to display God's power.

The frustrated Philistines finally recruited someone to betray him. Samson took the bait and set himself up for a humiliating fall. Because of that his story didn't end well, but he still stands as an example of how God can work in a person's life and enable them to do extraordinary things.

Then Peter, filled with the Holy Spirit, said to them: "Rulers and elders of the people!" (Acts 4:8)

Peter is one of my favorite characters in the Bible. The description of his courageous witness in Acts 4 makes me wish I had been there to see it in person. I can just picture this former fisherman standing before the "rulers, the elders and the teachers of the law" (v. 5). He didn't let the obvious difference in their social standing deter him at all. He simply proceeded to tell them that salvation could be found in no other name than the name of Jesus. His boldness was not based on bravado or his own ego;

instead, it was based on all he had experienced with Jesus and then fueled by the Holy Spirit.

Peter's faithfulness and courage continued to grow. He learned what it meant to minister without Jesus physically by his side but in the power of God's Spirit. By the end of Peter's life, he had gone to Rome and confronted the most powerful people of his generation with the truth of the gospel. Why? Because he chose to believe that Jesus of Nazareth was God's Son, and he wanted to see His kingdom extended on the earth. Acting on that desire, Peter allowed himself to be filled and used by the Holy Spirit to accomplish great things.

God's Power on My Doorstep?

However, as it is written:

> "What no eye has seen,
> what no ear has heard,
> and what no human mind has conceived"—
> the things God has prepared for those who
> love him—

these are the things God has revealed to us by his Spirit. (1 Corinthians 2:9–10)

The internet has dramatically changed how we shop. Once upon a time our selection was limited by the items in a catalog. We would review a few pictures, place a call, and within a week or so our purchases would arrive. Shopping is quite different today. The internet delivers an almost limitless set of choices. But it isn't just the huge selection of products that has changed our habits;

it's the way sellers have solved the logistical problems. When we were able to see something online and then have that something on our doorstep within hours, our expectations about buying and selling changed forever.

Many of us have a complete doctrine of God but an incomplete experience of God. We've read in the Bible about the things God used to do, but we had no imagination they could come to our doorsteps. It is almost as if we are reviewing a catalog of the ways God used to interact with His people. Unfortunately, too often we conclude that those activities are not unfolding today. In fact, some churches have seminars about when those things stopped and why they no longer happen. We're fine with talking about the supernatural movement of God, but we're not sure that we're prepared to experience it. We have settled for a historical Jesus but do not embrace His commandment to cooperate with the Holy Spirit. That's because we've left the Holy Spirit out of the equation.

The Holy Spirit is the One who helps us understand, and benefit from, the redemptive work of Jesus. He is the person God chose for distributing His power and His blessings to humanity. Today we desperately need a relationship with the Spirit of God. We need to throw our doors wide open and welcome Him into every corner of our lives. When we approach Him with a welcoming attitude, we allow the power of God, the blessings of God, the intent of God, to fill our lives.

Making the Holy Spirit Welcome

> Now about the gifts of the Spirit, brothers and sisters, I do not want you to be uninformed. (1 Corinthians 12:1)

Before Jesus left the earth, He gathered His disciples and gave them some final instructions. One point stood above the rest: the Holy Spirit would come to help Jesus' followers, and the Spirit would be with us forever. Paul's letters to the Corinthians show that he understood the significance of the Spirit's presence and how the gifts of the Spirit could impact followers of Jesus.

Few topics bring more anxiety and division to the people of God than a discussion of the Holy Spirit. We'll say that we want to welcome Him, but we back away pretty quickly when it comes to practical expressions of that. I invite you to welcome the Holy Spirit into your life—to acknowledge Him as your Helper, to become familiar with Him, to recognize His voice, to understand His promptings, and to heed His warnings. God's gift of the Holy Spirit is absolutely necessary to our well-being—why would we not want His help in every part of our lives?

I am more aware than I have ever been of my need for the Holy Spirit. The redemptive work of Jesus is an accomplished fact—nothing can be added to it, and nothing can be taken from it. But understanding that gift of redemption and implementing it fully are possible only with the help of the Holy Spirit.

The thought that the Spirit of the almighty God would want to know me and participate in my life is an incredibly humbling thing. Why would He do that? I am inconsistent, even on my best day, yet He is ready to help whenever I turn to Him. He is my friend, and I want to make sure He is an everyday part of my life. I want to welcome Him into my thoughts and behaviors more than ever before.

When it comes to the things of God, it seems to me that many of us try to find a way to straddle the fence. We don't want to be offensive to nonbelievers. We don't want to be seen as too religious. So we try to find a safe place on the fence and watch the action from there. But when we invite the Holy Spirit to truly work in our lives, He sends an electric current through that fence and makes it an uncomfortable place to sit. When we give the Holy Spirit more room to work in our hearts, we experience the changes that He brings and have a desire for more of Him. My prayer is that we would express an increasing willingness to embrace the person of the Holy Spirit. I invite you to climb down from the fence and say to the Holy Spirit, "You are welcome in my life." How do we do that?

Take down the barriers and open the floodgates. "Jesus stood and said in a loud voice, 'Let anyone who is thirsty come to me and drink. Whoever believes in me, as the Scripture has said, rivers of living water will flow from within them.' By this he meant the Spirit, whom those who believed in him were later to receive" (John 7:37–39). Israel is predominantly a desert country, and it's very easy to become dehydrated there. Jesus' audience would have been well aware of their need for water, so it was natural for Him to compare that need with their need for the Holy Spirit.

I've been extremely hot and thirsty many times in my life. Bush-hogging a field during a Tennessee summer and hiking in a desert in Israel are a couple of situations that come to mind. I imagine you've experienced extreme thirst too. And I imagine that when water became available, you didn't care too much about your manners. You probably didn't ask to be served in a pretty crystal glass. You probably put that hose or cup or bottle to your mouth and started gulping as fast as you could. And you may have poured some over your head!

I encourage you to lay down your preconceived notions about the Holy Spirit. Do not put up any barriers or make any exceptions about where and when He is welcome and how you will allow Him to work in your life. Ask Him for the "rivers of living water" that only He can supply, and drink them like the thirsty person you are. Once you taste that life-giving water, you will never thirst for anything else!

FRUIT OF THE SPIRIT AND GIFTS OF THE SPIRIT

Now to each one the manifestation of the Spirit is given for the common good. To one there is given through the Spirit a message of wisdom, to another a message of knowledge by means of the same Spirit, to another faith by the same Spirit, to another gifts of healing by that one Spirit, to another miraculous powers, to another prophecy, to another distinguishing between spirits, to another speaking in different kinds of tongues, and to still another the interpretation of tongues. All these are the work of one and the same Spirit, and he distributes them to each one, just as he determines. (1 Corinthians 12:7–12)

But the fruit of the Spirit is love, joy, peace, forbearance, kindness, goodness, faithfulness, gentleness and self-control. . . . Since we live by the Spirit, let us keep in step with the Spirit. (Galatians 5:22–23, 25)

The gifts of the Spirit and the fruit of the Spirit are different, but they are both expressions of the power of the Spirit of God.

I think of the fruit of the Spirit as the insulation that enables us to give expression to the gifts of the Spirit. The fruit of the Spirit is made evident in our character formation. The gifts of the Spirit are demonstrations of God's power. Sometimes God's desire to help His people is so great He will speak through a donkey (see the story of Balaam in Numbers 22:21–39). However, to consistently live in the power of the Spirit, we must cooperate with the Holy Spirit and be transformed into the image of Jesus—and that is about change from the inside out.

One way to think about the difference between the gifts of the Spirit and the fruit of the Spirit is to picture the difference between a Christmas tree and an apple tree.

The gifts of the Spirit are like a Christmas tree. Imagine a beautiful tree covered with lights and decorations. No one sees that tree and thinks, "Look at what a healthy tree that is. It grew lights and decorations!" Everyone understands that the lights and decorations do not reflect anything the tree has done for itself. Someone did that for the tree. When you see the gifts of the Spirit in someone's life, you see gifts that God has lovingly bestowed on that person.

The fruit of the Spirit, on the other hand, is like an apple tree. You see it covered with beautiful apples, and you recognize that the fruit demonstrates the health and vitality of that tree. When you see the fruit of the Spirit evident in people's lives, you know they have chosen to yield themselves to the Spirit and let the character of God be formed in them.

All of these things are expressions of the grace of God and the power of God. They help us interact with our world, flourish in our world, demonstrate that there is a God, and sustain His church. We need all of these things to complete what God has called us to, and I believe each of them is still fully at work in our world today.

THE SPIRIT AT WORK IN YOU

Have you ever used a circular saw? Mine is an extremely efficient tool that cuts through a variety of materials, depending on the blade I'm using. That saw is very powerful—as long as it is connected to its power source. When it is plugged in, the blade moves about 120 miles per hour and makes quick work of many tasks. When it is not plugged in, it is a lifeless hunk of metal. It has potential power, but without being plugged in it is not very helpful. We will not flourish in the season ahead without being connected to the power of God. No matter what intellectual and physical capacity you have, and what has been invested in you personally and professionally, if you are disconnected from your power source you will never know what your true potential is. You will never know what you could have become or what you could have done. The Spirit of God is your power source, and only with His help will you become and accomplish all that you are designed for.

The Spirit of God doesn't move in our lives because we earn it or deserve it. The Holy Spirit is God's gift to us, and He moves in our lives in spite of our fallen nature. My experience and observation is that the more you learn to welcome Him and cooperate with Him, and the more you allow the fruit of the Spirit to grow and flourish in your life, the more frequently the Holy Spirit expresses Himself in power through your life in a multitude of ways.

The presence of the Spirit of God and the power of God have not diminished across the span of history, no matter the context. If you give yourself to the Lord, there will be people who will watch and wonder, "I know that person, and I don't understand how that could happen." Then you will be able to say, "Let me tell you what the Lord has done for me!"

The church in every generation needs to understand the fullness of what Jesus did on the cross, and that will be possible only with the help of the Holy Spirit. We no longer have the luxury of quibbling about subtle differences in the practice of our faith. We need one another, and we need to stand together in the truth of God and the unity of the Spirit so that we can bring glory and honor to Jesus in our world today.

I wholeheartedly agree with what Paul wrote to the Romans: "If God is for us, who can be against us?" (8:31). If God is for us, and He is, then He is capable of opening doorways to things that we could not have imagined for ourselves. We must learn to believe in the possibilities of God, the forgiveness that Jesus offers, and the power of the Holy Spirit to help us live out God's plans and purposes. Believe that God is for you. Believe that He wants good things for you and that nothing is impossible for Him.

I'm not interested in playing church, and I pray that you aren't either. If there is a God, and if Jesus is His Son, and if His Spirit is present with us today, let's give ourselves without reservation to telling His story and cooperating with Him in every way. Let's stand together under the banner of the cross and present a unified witness to the world.

PRAYER

Heavenly Father, we ask that You would give us the Spirit of wisdom and revelation that we might know You better. We pray that the eyes of our hearts may be enlightened in order that we may know the hope to which You have called us, the riches of our glorious inheritance in the saints, and Your incomparably great power for us who believe. Come, Holy Spirit. You are welcome in our lives. Give us eyes to see and ears to hear—we choose to cooperate with You. Grant us a revelation of the living God. Help us to honor Jesus of Nazareth in this generation. Give us understanding of God's provision for our lives—His love, His great power expressed toward us and through us. May the hope of the living God surround us today. In Jesus' name, amen.

CHAPTER 7

THE PATH OF THE STORM

The Pharisees and Sadducees came to Jesus and tested him by asking him to show them a sign from heaven. He replied, "When evening comes, you say, 'It will be fair weather, for the sky is red,' and in the morning, 'Today it will be stormy, for the sky is red and overcast.' You know how to interpret the appearance of the sky, but you cannot interpret the signs of the times."

—MATTHEW 16:1–3

The weather where I live in Middle Tennessee is pretty predictable. Even though we are a long way from the tropics, our climate is classified as "humid subtropical." Winter is cool and wet with a few really cold days. Christmas Day is just as likely to call for sandals as it is for snow boots. Spring is warm and wet. We're sneezing through clouds of pollen and headed for our favorite garden centers. Summer is hot and humid. We're wilting and dripping and drinking iced tea. Fall is cooler and less humid with beautiful changing leaves. And we're all rejoicing!

But sometimes we have a weather event that is life-changing. That can come in the form of a thunderstorm with damaging straight-line winds or significant rainfall that causes serious and often dangerous flooding. But most of our life-changing weather events are tornadoes. In fact, Tennessee has the largest percentage of tornadoes that result in fatalities in the United States.[1]

I like to poke fun at the shortcomings of weather prognostication, but sometimes it is very helpful and even lifesaving. A local meteorologist can tell me when the conditions are right for a tornado to form in my area, when a confirmed tornado is in the air or on the ground, and if a tornado is headed for my street.

So when the conditions are right for a tornado to head my way, I won't trust my instincts to tell me if one is coming. I won't put my wife and myself at unnecessary risk during tornado season. I'll look for help from those people who have access to cutting-edge technology.

Just as there are atmospheric conditions that contribute to the development of physical storms, there are cultural conditions that contribute to the development of spiritual storms. We've been seeing those conditions gathering around us for some time, and the storm season has already begun. In fact, there are storms on the ground and barreling down our streets. Lawlessness, increasing violence, censorship of ideas in the public square, redefining family and marriage—the list of disruptive and destructive forces is long.

I don't say this because I want to frighten you. Nor do I want to incite anger toward anyone or any group. I say this because I believe God is moving in the earth and Satan is expressing his hatred for all those who love God. That combination makes for a turbulent world.

In the above passage from Matthew 16, we see Jesus reprimanding the religious leaders for their lack of interest in spiritual things. Just as He wanted them to take notice of what was happening around them spiritually, He wants us to be awake and aware of what is going on in the world around us. When we are awake and aware, we will be able to respond to whatever comes in a godly, informed way.

> When we are awake and aware, we will be able to respond to whatever comes in a godly, informed way.

FORECAST FOR TODAY AND TOMORROW: STORMS

We have had storm clouds blowing around us for some time now, and most of the problems were here long before COVID-19 was identified. The things the pandemic brought to light had been lurking in the shadows before, and while we're learning to manage the physical threat of COVID-19, I think some of the threats we face today are perhaps greater.

What's happening now is far more spiritual. And just as a physical storm watch is updated on a regular basis, our spiritual storm watch needs to be updated regularly because the storms we faced two years ago and one year ago are not the same storms we are facing today. Let's look at some of the storms that are gathering in the world around us.

Anemic Theology and a Threatened Church

The church is not a building or a denomination. The church is about Jesus of Nazareth. He is the incarnate Son of God and the head of the church. He led a sinless life in obedience to His Father. He died on a cross for our sins, then was buried and raised to life again. God's love, God's mercy, God's grace, and God's judgment are all understood in the context of Jesus' life and redemptive work and eventual return at the end of the age. These are central to the theology of the church.

There are congregations and denominations that have left behind the triune God of the Bible and the truth of the Bible in favor of a deity and a theology they have crafted in their own image and liking. This is heartbreaking because many of them were theologically sound at their beginning.

Without that complete story of Jesus, a church is not the church. I don't care what the architecture looks like or what the sign says. I don't care how religious the language sounds or how enthusiastic the participants are. It's not the church unless Jesus is at its head.

The church also is being buffeted from outside its walls. As the culture has coarsened, the church is often seen as the enemy. And our enemy, Satan, must have been cackling with glee when he saw churches being shuttered due to COVID-19. Unfortunately, the church has not stood up for its beliefs about God and the changes for good He can make in people's lives.

Jesus warned us we would be hated because of our affiliation with Him. Resistance and hatred should not cause us to cower in fear or to negotiate with evil. We can ask for boldness and wisdom to be ambassadors in this pivotal season. God has given us everything we need for life and godliness.

The Problem with Misremembering

Truth is caught in the pathway of this storm, and I don't mean just biblical truth; I mean the public expression of truth. There was a time when truth was held in high esteem in the public square, but that is no longer the case. Truth is not highly regarded, even at the highest levels of our nation.

We are seeing the dissemination of propaganda wrapped in the cloak of legitimate news and information—and that's from some of the most respected and trusted sources in our country. This is happening even as censorship is promoted and excused as right and necessary for the common good.

Words matter, but we're redefining words and creating new words to diminish our awareness of truth. We have a whole new vocabulary to justify lying. We spin the truth. We manage the truth. We interpret the truth. We misspeak. We misremember. If you put on your résumé that you graduated from Harvard when in fact you graduated from Hometown U, you did not "misremember" that!

Deception is going to escalate, but we can avoid being deceived if we hold everything we hear up to the light of Scripture and focus on maintaining a biblical worldview.

The Courage to Speak: Truth and Consequences

Our system of freedoms is built on our right to freedom of speech, and we've tolerated some very offensive things in order to demonstrate our commitment to it. But freedom of speech is not just for those who produce pornography or spout profanity or burn the flag or kneel when our national anthem is played. It's intended for all of us.

I understand that freedom of speech is protected by the First

Amendment of our Constitution, but it has been pulled from beneath us as we stood by and watched. Censorship of ideas and prohibitions of speech in government, in business, in schools, in the media, and on social media have become so commonplace that we're not even surprised anymore.

Isaiah wrote, "Truth has stumbled in the streets, honesty cannot enter. Truth is nowhere to be found, and whoever shuns evil becomes a prey" (Isaiah 59:14–15). Today if you publicly express a biblical perspective toward immorality and say, "I don't approve of that," you will become prey for the voices promoting those things. If you speak God's truth, many will try to drown you out, discredit you, ostracize you, or even take you to court.

This "cancel culture," which does not welcome a free exchange of diverse opinions, has resulted in a stunning silence from the people of God. We're going to have to find our voices and the resolve to stand up and speak. Let that desire begin in your heart. It will require courage, but the Holy Spirit will give you the strength you need to stand for righteousness.

The Government Has No Money

America was founded on the shoulders of capitalism. Capitalism focuses on private ownership, competitive markets, a price system, private property, and the recognition of property rights. But if it's not tempered by other factors, such as humility and charity, it can lead to the conclusion that the one with the most money is the winner.

For many years there has been talk in our country about the supposed benefits of socialism. We think of socialism mostly in terms of economics and how we manage resources, and how

THE PATH OF THE STORM

they're distributed or redistributed. Known for its guaranteed income and "free" housing, health care, education, and daycare, it is a thoroughly unsuccessful concept that has failed miserably in the countries where it has been implemented.[2]

Socialism's advocates say that socialism could flourish in a democracy with some degree of personal liberty and freedom. Increasingly authoritarian attitudes suggest a shift toward Marxist expressions of power. Marxism openly uses domination and manipulation to gain control of power structures, and that seems like a more accurate description of what we are seeing in America today. Its proponents do not like to acknowledge the fact that over one hundred million people died under the cruel hands of Marxism in the twentieth century.[3]

No matter the "isms" that are being promoted, we're definitely seeing the purposeful destruction of our economy. This has the effect of increasing dependence on the government and empowering central control over major segments of our lives. It is also cultivating a sense of dissatisfaction and fostering an attitude of entitlement. We're waiting for resources we didn't earn to be given to us by a government that doesn't earn money. The only money the government has to spend is what it takes from someone else and redistributes. Every time we take those unearned resources, we forfeit some independence.

The United States is the land of opportunity. That's been our story from the beginning, and it's the reason so many people from other countries want to come here. Instead of increasing dependence on the government, we should be talking about the value and dignity of hard work, the satisfaction of accomplishment, and the necessity of personal sacrifice in order to achieve success.

The Increase of Lawlessness

The rule of law is being challenged all around us, and there are very few voices speaking against it. Violence and crime are exploding across our nation, fueled by sin and a whole host of resulting social ills. Incredibly, some local governments have decided to reduce the penalties for criminal behavior. "Smash and grab" has replaced "looting" and "armed robbery" in our lexicon. Another counterintuitive result of rising violence and crime was a mounting chorus to defund the police.

That is nothing more than short-sighted rebellion against authority. Police officers aren't perfect, and I'm not saying that to excuse anyone's bad behavior. But we cannot abolish authority and think that we will live in peace. It is no surprise that crime rates soar where the law enforcement presence is diminished. You don't need a PhD in social science to understand the faultiness and foolishness of that logic.

Law enforcement officers at all levels have been ridiculed, mocked, and held up to scorn and derision. I hope that when you see them, you will thank them for their service. Their assignment before God is to make decisions that will promote godliness and give us the freedom to be advocates for the gospel of Jesus. I encourage you to pray for them on a regular basis and pray that God will bring godly persons into those places of authority. Because without the rule of law, our society will crumble.

The Chaos from an Open Border

Our immigration crisis, which is focused mainly on our southern border, is of great concern to the American people but is not a priority for our elected representatives.[4] Seventy-five percent of Americans believe that the United States is a nation of immigrants, and I am pro-immigrant.[5] I agree that our immigration policies need to be changed, but we need to do that legally because we won't survive as an independent and free nation with open borders.

We shouldn't pretend unregulated immigration isn't a problem, because to suspend our laws and open our borders is a commitment to lawlessness that cannot be undone. Our broken immigration system has resulted in cities, counties, and states that have declared themselves sanctuaries from federal immigration law—but they still demand federal funding.[6] If we can suspend one law to suit one group of people, who will decide which law is suspended next?

Some people argue that having open borders is an expression of compassion and will help solve the problem of global poverty, but that is wishful thinking. Billions of people around the world live in poverty, and the relatively small numbers that we can assimilate into our nation will not change that. In addition to people who are seeking a better life, we have illegal drugs and both perpetrators and victims of human trafficking entering our country. These and other problems will not be solved by porous borders. That will require proclaiming the name of Jesus throughout the earth and encouraging believers to adopt a Christian worldview that will transform their lives and their cultures.

Who Defines Morality?

Immorality is being expressed in brazen ways and escalating to a degree that I could never have imagined. Let's look at some of the fronts of this particular storm.

The Nuclear Family. We are seeing a very purposeful and unrelenting effort to destroy the nuclear family. The notion of family as a married man and woman and their biological children in the home is not an easy ideal to hold. It's enormous work, but it's the most stable, healthy way for humans to live. That was shown in the pages of Scripture and has been proven across the span of history.

Our culture has allowed marriage to be redefined, as if that changes reality. God established marriage between a man and a woman, and His definition of marriage has never changed. No matter what the culture tells you, don't allow yourself to be deceived about what marriage is.

Decency. Decency was in the news several years ago as media organizations and watchdog groups debated what language and behavior was decent. It wasn't really a question of what was decent or indecent; it was a question of what the culture was willing to allow. We have since allowed our standards to become so low that pornography and extreme violence have become mainstream entertainment.

Hollywood makes what we will pay to see. If we will change our hearts and no longer pay to see ungodly entertainment, Hollywood will no longer have an incentive to produce it. Ask the Holy Spirit for a new sense of discernment about the media you consume. Determine to lay ungodliness aside and begin to honor the Lord with every aspect of your life.

Sexuality. Marriage is completely irrelevant in many circles, so the Bible's prohibition of sex outside of marriage seems quaint and outdated to much of the population. This is an area where people either ignore God's instructions or twist them to suit their own desires. God's opinion on this hasn't changed, however. I assume that if it does, He will let us know!

And perhaps no topic occupies current discussions more

than gender. My dad was a veterinarian, and I grew up in fields and barns. Trust me—gender is not that confusing. If persons are confused about their gender, we should respond with compassion. But we don't want to invite our children into that confusion and expose them to its destructive influences.

Public Indoctrination Systems

The American education system began in order to prepare young people to take their place in their homes and in society and lead when they became adults. It has been transformed into an opportunity for indoctrination. Schools are no longer focused on teaching students *how* to think but on telling them *what* to think. Since godly precepts have been banished from public schools, what they are told to think looks increasingly like an exercise in social engineering.

Many private schools are even farther down this path than public schools. And I am sad to say that many so-called Christian schools have fallen into this trap as well. The desire on the part of many administrations and many parents is to fit in with popular culture rather than to stand for the truth of the Bible.

HOW SHOULD WE RESPOND?

My Bible says that God will never ask you to walk through something without giving you everything you need to walk through it triumphantly. So wherever you find yourself, God has equipped you to meet those challenges.

I do think that the storm raging around us right now is greater than any we have faced in my lifetime. But I don't think this is a permanent condition. Right now, we are feeling the effects of sustained winds and storm surges. But there is an ebb and flow to storms, and it remains to be seen how long this storm will last and what its effects will be.

> Wherever you find yourself, God has equipped you to meet those challenges.

The storm conditions that are around us can put us at tremendous risk, but they also can provide us with tremendous opportunities. In the passage from Matthew at the beginning of this chapter, Jesus called the religious leaders to account for their lack of spiritual awareness. And in Luke He asked the same of everyone else:

He said to the crowd: "When you see a cloud rising in the west, immediately you say, 'It's going to rain,' and it does. And when the south wind blows, you say, 'It's going to be hot,' and it is. Hypocrites! You know how to interpret the appearance of the earth and the sky. How is it that you don't know how to interpret this present time?" (Luke 12:54–56)

Jesus is calling us to open our eyes and be aware—culturally aware and spiritually aware. There are some fierce things being unleashed on humanity in this season. Certainly, history has seen terrible things, but there is a bold aggressiveness to the evil we are seeing that is unprecedented in my lifetime. There's a destructive character to it at the fundamental, foundational level of human society. We are opening the doorway to some things that only the power of God can reverse, and what that will mean for the generations who follow us is impossible to know.

We've seen that we are in the path of a storm. There is trouble around us and more trouble ahead of us. That is why our role is critical. That is why we must have more than head knowledge of the gospel of Jesus Christ. We must know the message and the power of the gospel on an experiential level and bring it to bear on the issues we face. We must be ready to talk about it and patiently use it to correct, rebuke, and encourage—not just from the pulpits of our country, but in our homes, schools, workplaces, and every other area of our lives.

CHAPTER 8

GETTING READY

So prepare your minds for action and exercise self-control. Put all your hope in the gracious salvation that will come to you when Jesus Christ is revealed to the world. So you must live as God's obedient children. Don't slip back into your old ways of living to satisfy your own desires. You didn't know any better then. But now you must be holy in everything you do, just as God who chose you is holy. For the Scriptures say, "You must be holy because I am holy."

—1 PETER 1:13–16 NLT

"MAY I HAVE YOUR ATTENTION, PLEASE?"

Flight attendants have to be prepared for many different kinds of challenging situations, and they want their passengers to be prepared for some of them too. A flight attendant's instructions about possible turbulence will always include something like this:

If needed, oxygen masks will be released overhead. To start the flow of oxygen, reach up and pull the mask toward you, fully extending the plastic tubing. Place the mask over your nose and mouth and slip the elastic band over your head. To tighten the fit, pull the tab on each side of the mask. The plastic bag does not need to inflate when oxygen is flowing. Be sure to secure your own mask before assisting others.[1]

> We should be getting ourselves spiritually prepared so that we'll be able to help other people when they need us.

That last sentence—"Be sure to secure your own mask before assisting others"—is very important. After all, you won't be much help to someone else if you don't have oxygen yourself!

This principle applies to the Christian life as well. We're in a stormy season. We're already experiencing turbulence, and there is more ahead. We should be getting ourselves spiritually prepared so that we'll be able to help other people when they need us. How do we do that?

CHOOSE WHOM YOU WILL SERVE

Joshua is known for many things, but perhaps he is best known for being chosen by God to take over from Moses and lead His people into the promised land. Joshua was devoted to God and wanted the Israelites to be devoted to Him as well. Joshua 24 documents the last time God's people gathered before Joshua's death, and he had some final things to say to them. He knew these were his last words for God's people, and he wanted to make them count.

He began by describing all that God had done for their ancestors. Then he reminded them that God had brought them and their parents out of generations of slavery and taken care of their every need in the wilderness. Next he detailed God's generosity to the current generation.

And then came this challenge and declaration:

> Now fear the LORD and serve him with all faithfulness. Throw away the gods your ancestors worshiped beyond the Euphrates River and in Egypt, and serve the LORD. But if serving the LORD seems undesirable to you, then choose for yourselves this day whom you will serve, whether the gods your ancestors served beyond the Euphrates, or the gods of the Amorites, in whose land you are living. But as for me and my household, we will serve the LORD. (Joshua 24:14–15)

The Israelites had lived as slaves to their Egyptian masters for four hundred years before their deliverance. They had a long cultural memory of the Egyptians' idol worship, and they knew that Abraham had been called by God out of a pagan family.

We tend to define our faith based on how our grandparents or our parents worshiped, and it can feel very frightening to step beyond the boundaries of that. God had to continually remind them that they were His chosen people and that He was their only God. Here Joshua reminded them of that yet again, and he asked them to make a choice: Would they serve almighty God? Or would they serve some other god?

You may recognize "As for me and my household, we will serve the Lord" from its display in many Christian homes. A quick internet search found it inscribed on wall plaques, flags, clocks, cutting boards, doormats, shower curtains, pillows, license plate holders, and fake rocks! But I hope it is more than a church-y, feel-good saying for you. I hope it is the deepest desire of your heart.

You see, I encounter many people with an inherited faith. For those of us who grew up where Christianity is the norm, we might think that officially "becoming a Christian" is something everyone does—or at least what our parents and grandparents did and what is expected of us too. Made a profession of faith? Check. Said the sinner's prayer? Check. Got dunked in water? Check. Ticket to heaven punched? Check!

> Following Jesus is a personal, lifelong journey of walking with the Lord and learning to know Him better.

But following Jesus is much more than that. It is a personal, lifelong journey of walking with the Lord and learning to know Him better. It is allowing Him to transform you from the inside out. If you have not already done so, I pray that you will commit yourself to following Jesus and allowing Him to change you. I hope that your faith will become more than a "family thing." I hope that knowing the Lord deeply and serving Him all of your days will become the deepest longing of your heart.

And part of that process will be identifying the things we have made into gods and throwing them away, either mentally or physically or both. Some of us have allowed our hobbies and pastimes to become the priorities of our lives. Some of us have adopted philosophies and practices from Eastern religions. Some of us look to our horoscope or a psychic or a palm reader. Some of us are into yoga or meditation or martial arts that are based on Eastern religions. Saying, "Oh, that's just for fun" or "I do it for the exercise" won't protect you from the destruction you're inviting into your life. Some of us have taken pagan gods so lightly that we have artwork or statues of them sitting in our homes and gardens. Over and over, the Bible tells us not to worship or make graven images of other gods. I urge you with all seriousness to do a personal and household inventory and rid your heart, mind, schedule, and home of anything that hints of pagan idolatry.

Life is completely different when we truly make Jesus our Lord. Accepting Jesus as Savior is a necessary first step. But when we acknowledge Him as Lord of our lives, His values, His choices, and His perspectives take first place and become our priority. This decision is not a complicated one that requires great theological expertise. It is a simple commitment to intentionally seek the Lord and honor Him every day.

COME ON IN!

Have you ever heard of "perpetual students"? These are people who love learning and the safety of the academic environment so much that they would rather stay there, taking class after class and earning degree after degree, than take their education out into the world and put it to practical use.

I think that many of us are like that—perpetual students of Christianity. We enjoy reading and studying and discussing our faith in a theoretical way, but we find it challenging to take it into the world and put it into action. However, that is exactly what the Lord wants of us.

Paul wrote, "All Scripture is God-breathed and is useful for teaching, rebuking, correcting and training in righteousness, so that the servant of God may be thoroughly equipped for every good work" (2 Timothy 3:16–17). The often-quoted first part of this passage—"All Scripture is God-breathed and is useful for teaching, rebuking, correcting and training in righteousness"— has a punchline that we don't hear quite as often: "so that the servant of God may be thoroughly equipped for every good work."

It requires a much higher level of commitment to put the teachings of Scripture into action than to sit in a group and talk about them, but that is what we're called to do. God wants us to set ourselves apart for His purposes and then allow Him to use us to change the world.

Another group of us are cultural Christians. These are the people who live with so much peace and affluence that it is possible to be content while wading in the shallow end of God's kingdom. Folks simply go through the steps that are necessary to join the church their family and friends are a part of without really knowing what they believe or why. Church participation is focused more on going along with the crowd and fulfilling cultural expectations than on awakening and facilitating a lifelong spiritual transformation.

But God is inviting us out of the shallow end of the pool. He is like my father, who stood in water well over my young head and urged me to trust him and jump into the adventure and safety of his arms. God is inviting us to open our hearts fully to Him and dive deeply into His plans and purposes. Will that always be easy? No. Will that always be fun? No. Will there be opposition? I'm certain of it. But God is in the business of purifying His church and creating for Himself a holy people, a royal priesthood who revere and worship Him in every aspect of our lives. He is watching over us, and we should be willing to trust Him and joyfully participate in His purposes in the earth.

"CONSECRATE YOURSELVES"

In Joshua 3 we read a story of God's faithful provision in a seemingly impossible situation. The Israelites were preparing to cross the Jordan River into the promised land, and they were unsure of what life on the other side would be like. But their more pressing concern was getting an entire nation of people across a river that was at flood stage and overflowing its banks. They seemingly had forgotten that God had already parted a sea for them, and they saw this as an engineering problem rather than a faith problem.

Joshua reminded them that God was more than capable of getting His chosen people across a river, and they should prepare themselves for a miracle: "Consecrate yourselves, for tomorrow the LORD will do amazing things among you" (Joshua 3:5). God showed once again that He is in control of the natural world. Priests carrying the ark of the covenant went first, and as soon as they set foot in the Jordan River, the water stopped flowing. "The priests who carried the ark of the covenant of the LORD stopped in the middle of the Jordan and stood on dry ground, while all Israel passed by until the whole nation had completed the crossing on dry ground" (Joshua 3:17).

Joshua's message is just as relevant for us today. The greatest breakthroughs in our lives come when we submit ourselves to God's direction, cooperate with Him, and expect Him to do great things. Are you willing to set yourself apart for the purposes of God? He can make miraculous things a part of your future, but the choice will be yours. He will invite you, but He won't beg you, or bribe you, or force you. You and I will have to choose to set ourselves apart in order to fulfill the plans He has for us. How do we get ourselves ready to be used by God?

SHIELD YOURSELF FROM THE ENEMY

Peter wrote, "Be alert and of sober mind. Your enemy the devil prowls around like a roaring lion looking for someone to devour. Resist him, standing firm in the faith" (1 Peter 5:8–9). The presence of pure evil in the world is something we'd rather not think about. But the stark reality is that you have a spiritual adversary who intends to obstruct God's purposes for your life, and he has a kingdom of associates who will help him in that task.

We don't know all of Satan's story, but we do know that he was an angel who wanted to be worshiped as God was worshiped. Satan led a rebellion against God, and God cast him and a third of the angels out of heaven. Ever since, he has been at work on the earth trying to get humanity to worship him.

Sometimes we think we are too sophisticated to believe in the devil, but Jesus had firsthand knowledge of him and knew how destructive he could be (Matthew 4:1–11). Commit yourself to vigilance by being self-controlled and alert. Always being on guard doesn't sound like fun, but the peace you will feel will be worth it. Guard your heart. Choose your friends wisely. Be intentional about how you spend your discretionary time. Make a habit of Bible reading and prayer, and you will gradually find it easier to recognize and resist evil when it touches your life. Do not give the Enemy an inch when he attempts to gain a foothold. The power you have through the blood of Jesus and the wisdom available to you through God's Word and the leading of the Holy Spirit are greater than any power that wants to destroy you.

PURSUE HOLINESS

One of the consistent messages of the Bible is that God wants us to pursue holiness. In the Old Testament, God gave His covenant people the Ten Commandments and the Mosaic law as rules to help them stay morally and ritually pure. In the New Testament, we are offered a new way to be reconciled to God by believing that Jesus is the Messiah and serving Him as our Lord and King. We pursue holiness by following Jesus' example and allowing the Holy Spirit to work to transform us from the inside out. Then we will reflect His holiness to the world.

Holiness is a pretty intimidating topic; actually, it seems like an unattainable goal. After all, only God is truly holy. And the concept of holiness contradicts every value judgment that our society places great store in. But God created us to be holy. In the same way that He designed us to breathe air and drink water, He designed us with a capacity for holiness. So if you're breathing, you have the capacity you need from the Creator to reflect the holiness of a living God.

The writer of Hebrews said that this should be a lifelong

priority for any follower of Jesus: "Make every effort to live in peace with everyone and to be holy; without holiness no one will see the Lord" (Hebrews 12:14). Make "every effort," he said. Not a half-hearted effort or an occasional effort—every effort. That means whatever the cost, whatever the inconvenience it may cause, whatever changes we must make, we are to do everything within our ability to live in peace with one another and be holy.

Holiness is a principle of action, not simply an abstract virtue of the soul or a theory to be set on a shelf and admired from afar. It is a standard that should determine not only our thoughts but our everyday behaviors as well. We don't keep the law to be holy; we keep our hearts pure to be holy. We set boundaries for ourselves. We put some fences around our emotions, attitudes, and behaviors. We forgive. We put a bridle on our tongues. We choose godliness when there are many voices telling us to choose ungodliness. We set apart time to spend with God and in His Word. Why? Because without holiness no one will see the Lord.

> Every one of us will struggle with holiness—ungodliness is our default position.

Every one of us will struggle with holiness—ungodliness is our default position. But the Holy Spirit, called "the Spirit of holiness" (Romans 1:4 NASB), will help us with this. Ask Him to help you reflect Jesus' character more fully at home, at work, and with your friends. This is His desire for you, and He will gladly show you what to do.

ACCEPT GOD'S DISCIPLINE

Have you ever been around a family where the parents exercised no control over their children? Everyone is utterly miserable, even the children who seem to be getting everything they want and everything their way. Scripture says that providing loving discipline is a sign of a caring parent: "Do not despise the LORD's discipline, and do not resent his rebuke, because the LORD disciplines those he loves, as a father the son he delights in" (Proverbs 3:11–12).

The Bible tells us on many occasions that God's boundaries are for our benefit, whether we feel like they are or not. It also says that when we bump up against one of His boundaries, we will experience His discipline—and that His discipline is a blessing! "Blessed is the one you discipline, LORD, the one you teach from your law" (Psalm 94:12).

I think we often learn those lessons the hard way. One summer I broke horses to earn money for college. I had spent years around horses by that time and wasn't afraid of them, even the angry ones. One night I was having trouble with a particularly difficult colt. He kept rearing up and striking at me, and one time I decided not to move out of the way. I'm not sure what I was trying to prove, but I took a hoof to the forehead and have a scar to show for it. It wasn't really the horse's fault. He was just being a horse, and he had been acting that way for about thirty minutes. It was my fault because there was an obvious boundary that I chose to ignore. I paid the price, but I also learned a valuable lesson.

When we choose to cooperate with the authority of Scripture and be trained by the boundaries that God gives us, His love will be made evident in those boundaries. In turn, His discipline will create things in us—holiness, righteousness, and peace—that we will benefit from.

Let's be honest with ourselves and admit that no one likes to be disciplined. We'd all like to skip over the hard parts and get the benefits without cooperating with the boundaries. But that is a part of the process of growing up as a follower of Jesus. When you step off God's path and feel His discipline, accept it for what it is—God's blessing—and learn everything you can from it.

FORGIVE

Unforgiveness is a heavy load to carry. It doesn't seem to bother the person who has transgressed; they usually carry on with few, if any, feelings of guilt. But for the person holding the grudge, it can be a cumbersome burden to bear. You see, unforgiveness carries with it a sense of indebtedness. We feel there was some injury suffered, and as a result we are owed something—an apology, restoration, or payback of some kind. Something must happen before we release this sense that our offender is in our debt.

Forgiveness says, "I release you. You don't owe me anything." Forgiveness does not mean justifying or excusing the actions of the offender. I'm just saying that unforgiveness is destructive, and it will choke out the purposes of God in your life. I meet people who experienced trauma many years ago but are still hanging on to feelings of bitterness and resentment and even rage. As a result, they are frozen in time and unable to move ahead with what God wants to do for them and through them.

One of the most astounding examples of forgiveness I have ever heard is that of Corrie ten Boom, who was sent to a concentration camp during World War II for helping Jewish people escape from the Nazis. At a speaking engagement after the war, she suddenly found herself face-to-face with a guard from the camp. He did not remember her, but she certainly remembered him. He had been among the cruelest of them all, and now he was a Christian, standing before her with his hand extended and asking for her forgiveness.

Even as she remembered his brutality and the lashes from the leather whip that had once hung from his belt, she did the hardest thing she had ever done: she put her hand into his. She wrote, "For a long moment we grasped each other's hands, the former guard and the former prisoner. I had never known God's love so intensely as I did then. But even so, I realized it was not my love. I had tried, and did not have the power. It was the power of the Holy Spirit."[2]

As Corrie ten Boom discovered, forgiveness is not an emotion; it is an active decision of your will. The choice to forgive is just as intentional as choosing to brush your teeth or feed your children or show up at your place of business. If you wait until you feel like forgiving, you'll probably never get there—you do it because God has instructed you to. When you decide to forgive, your emotions will catch up with your decision and you will be able to put down that heavy load.

The most astounding example of forgiveness in the Bible is when Jesus forgave the people who were executing Him. Hanging on a cross, He prayed, "Father, forgive them, for they do not know what they are doing" (Luke 23:34). It seems impossible that Jesus would forgive the people who were responsible for these unjust and cruel acts. But that is exactly what He did, and that is the example He left for us.

If you've been holding on to unforgiveness, I invite you to say, "God, I'm sorry. I've been bitter and filled with resentment. Please forgive me." If you'll take these simple steps of obedience, it will change the course of your life and open doors for God to work through you.

PUSH AWAY THAT FOOTREST

"The LORD had said to Abram, 'Go from your country, your people and your father's household to the land I will show you.' . . . Abram was seventy-five years old when he set out from Harran" (Genesis 12:1, 4). God came to Abram when he was past our traditional retirement age and said, "Let's go!" Abram accepted God's invitation without asking questions, and the rest is history—our history.

Later Caleb said, "Here I am today, eighty-five years old! I am still as strong today as the day Moses sent me out; I'm just as vigorous to go out to battle now as I was then. Now give me this hill country that the LORD promised me that day" (Joshua 14:10–12). Caleb was Joshua's right-hand man and an important part of the conquest of the promised land. But he had to wait forty-five years for the promise of God to be fulfilled in his life. Here he was, eighty-five years old, and he said, "I've got this. Give me an opportunity!"

If you are a tenured Christ follower, you may think that you've done all the significant things you're going to do in your life. You may have accomplished many of your life goals and checked a few things off your bucket list. You may think that now is your time to kick back and relax.

But that's not what the Bible teaches. If you have decided that it's time to put your feet up and sit on your good intentions, I invite you to push that footrest away and ask the Lord what He has for you to do. I don't think you're too old to participate in the advancement of His kingdom. In fact, I am confident that He has a plan and a purpose for every day of your life.

I invite you to purposefully, intentionally consider what God has called you to in this season. Churches and communities, families and individuals are in great need of the experience you have to offer. When you joyfully accept whatever assignment the Lord has for you—whether it's in your church, your community, or even in a land He will show you—you will be blessed as you bless others.

STAY THE COURSE

You've probably heard the saying, "Slow and steady wins the race." The origin of that adage is unclear, but it's believed to have sprung from Aesop's fable about the speedy but presumptuous hare being overtaken at the finish line by the slower but persistent tortoise.[3]

In *Good to Great*, Jim Collins wrote about how that principle applies to the business world. Through a study that tracked 1,435 companies over forty years, he and his team determined that the most successful companies hadn't had a unique idea or a fantastic marketing strategy; they simply clarified their objectives and pursued them intentionally over many years. Eventually, momentum took over and propelled them to outdistance the companies that were looking for something magical to happen.[4]

I think we want that kind of dramatic moment when it comes to spiritual things. We get discouraged if an angel hasn't brought us a message or God hasn't presented His plan on tablets of stone. My experience is that if you will walk in faith and earnestly seek the things of God, something will begin to happen. You'll look back in a year or two or three and realize that God has been doing something all along, something that perhaps once seemed impossible.

And no matter what happens, just keep putting one foot in front of the other. For example, did you know that over fifty people have walked across America? Some have done it just to prove that they could. Others have taken on the challenge to raise money or awareness of a cause. The incredible Bob Wieland walked on his hands after losing his legs during the Vietnam War. Amazing Doris Haddock traveled on cross-country skis the last hundred miles due to a snowstorm—and she was ninety at the time.[5] I think these people learned to set aside comfort and convenience in favor of perseverance, don't you?

The author of Hebrews told us to see our temporary discomforts from this perspective: "Consider him who endured such opposition from sinners, so that you will not grow weary and lose heart. In your struggle against sin, you have not yet resisted to the point of shedding your blood" (Hebrews 12:3–4). He was telling us that we should consider Jesus, who went ahead of us and endured far more than we are enduring. What are my temporary irritations compared to His death on the cross for me? Nothing in the Bible promises that the Christian life is easy or carefree. You are going to get tired and discouraged. But don't give in to those temporary emotions and give up. Whatever happens, just keep going!

Being God's people does not mean we're always given easy assignments. If you work or live in a hard place, or if you're the only Christian within shouting distance, consider that God may need you in that place for a season and He may have put you there specifically to be a light for Him. God will never ask you to stand in a place without giving you the strength to do so. He will allow you to carry burdens and face opposition, but when you persevere you will grow in your knowledge and experience of His faithfulness.

> God will never ask you to stand in a place without giving you the strength to do so.

If you're walking through a challenging season, I encourage you to stay the course. You haven't failed God, and God has not failed you. Neither is God punishing you. Instead, He has chosen you and trusted you with a difficult assignment. If you seek the Lord and follow the leadership of His Spirit, He will give you the strength you need to make a difference in your world. Count on it!

SOME THINGS TO THINK ABOUT

1. Is your faith in God something you inherited from your parents, or have you made it your own?
2. Have you allowed a hobby or pastime to encroach on your allegiance to the Lord?

3. Have you adopted any form or practice of a pagan religion and allowed it to creep into your spiritual life?

4. Do you find it easier to keep your faith in the realm of theory than to take it into the world and give it practical application?

5. Do you have a plan to shield yourself from the attacks of Satan, or do you play around with the world's temptations and hope for the best?

6. Do you have an action plan for pursuing holiness?

7. When you feel God's discipline, do you resent it or accept it and learn from it?

8. Are you burdened by the weight of unforgiveness, or have you chosen to forgive and set that load down?

9. Have you allowed your age to limit your responses to God's invitations?

10. Are you spiritually prepared to stay the course through a difficult season or assignment?

CHAPTER 9

WE ARE STRONGER TOGETHER

"Teacher," he asked, "what must I do to inherit eternal life?"
"What is written in the Law?" he replied. "How do you read it?" He
answered, "'Love the Lord your God with all your heart and with
all your soul and with all your strength and with all your mind'; and,
'Love your neighbor as yourself.'" "You have answered correctly,"
Jesus replied. "Do this and you will live."
—LUKE 10:25–28

The relative stability that defined most American lives before
2020 has been interrupted in drastic ways. The predictability of daily routines and seasonal activities. The belief that jobs would be there tomorrow. The certainty that churches would be open for worship and other activities. The assumption that

schools would be in session in their buildings. The confidence that stores would be doing business as usual and shelves would be stocked. The ability to plan a holiday celebration or a vacation. I'm sure you can think of many other things you took for granted that have changed in ways you never imagined.

I believe that God has initiated this massive interruption, this worldwide shaking, to awaken, purify, and strengthen His church. I believe that the shaking will continue and intensify until He comes again. The future has never been certain, of course, but I feel an urgency about it that I have never felt in my lifetime. Just as I want each of us to be prepared to meet the coming days with confidence, I want each of us to be prepared to help our neighbors face them as well.

We look at the world around us and think, "America needs to change!" I think more than any economic need we face, any medical need we face, any political changes we need, America needs a heart change. That's actually tremendously empowering, because heart changes can begin with us.

> God's people are at the center of what He is doing on the earth, and that includes you and me.

I believe that God's people are at the center of what He is doing on the earth, and that includes you and me. We have limited influence on medical research and international shipping, but we can have enormous influence if together we'll say, "We're going to make a difference in our world. And we're going to begin in our neighborhoods and communities."

In Jesus' parable of the good Samaritan (Luke 10:25–37), He

emphasized two things that are expected of us: we are to love God and love our neighbor. We understand loving God because we feel God's love for us and want to love Him in return. But what about our neighbors—people we may not even know, and people we do know but may not feel any particular affection for? That's a different thing altogether, isn't it? Let's explore what it means to love—and in turn, help—our neighbors.

FIRST THINGS FIRST!

The first thing I want us to think about is how to help our neighbors in a way that will be received. Have you ever had a conversation with a professional who used a specialized vocabulary that went completely over your head? It may have been a physician talking about your test results, a financial planner talking about your investment strategy, or a salesperson explaining all the features of a new television. At some point you may have said in frustration, "Will you please use words that I can understand?"

That applies to spiritual things too. We don't want to act like spiritual overachievers who have arrived and are waiting impatiently for the rest of the world to catch up with us. We also need to remember that adults are often reluctant to receive help, learn new things, think new thoughts, and form new habits. We need to take the time to understand where they are and meet them there.

Most important, we want them to know that we care about them, and we care about their relationship with Jesus because He can change their lives for the better. That being said, there are some stumbling blocks to these relationships. They have always been present, but some have been heightened by the anxiety of a global pandemic.

SOME OBSTACLES IN OUR PATH

Isolation and Fear

One of the things that the COVID-19 pandemic revealed is just how swiftly fear can overrule our common sense and how readily we will allow ourselves to be isolated. Voices of authority told us we should be very afraid, and we were. Those same voices told us we should isolate ourselves from the world as much as possible, and we did.

The voice of our Enemy amplified the confusion we were feeling and told us we should adopt a "survival of the fittest" mindset, and we complied. The scenes of panicked buying and selfish hoarding were terrible to witness. I saw one interview of a man who had just come out of a store and was visibly shaken by what he had experienced inside. "I don't know how to describe what I just saw in there," he said.

I don't have statistics to prove it, but I know that Christians, people who say they believe that God will provide for their needs, were in those stores frantically filling their carts too. They seem to have forgotten that Jesus told us again and again that He is our Provider and that we can depend on Him to meet our needs. In Luke 12:29–31 Jesus said, "And do not set your heart on what you will eat or drink; do not worry about it. For the pagan world runs after all such things, and your Father knows that you need them. But seek his kingdom, and these things will be given to you as well."

The cycle of isolation and fear and the selfishness that results is like a tenacious weed that is difficult to eradicate once it has taken root and spread its seeds. It will only be overcome by persistent expressions of love, concern, and compassion on the part of the people of God.

Skepticism

"The fool says in his heart, 'There is no God'" (Psalm 14:1). David wrote that many centuries ago, but that attitude is perhaps more fashionable than it has ever been. Haven't we become a little more aware, a little more appreciative of other religions? Why would we encumber ourselves by imagining there is only one holy, almighty God who created us, loves us, and deserves our complete loyalty? If you assert that there is a God who created the heavens and the earth, that you believe Jesus of Nazareth is His Son who died on a cross and was raised to life again, and that the Holy Spirit empowers us today, there will be a chorus of people who will say you are living in the unenlightened past.

There is no easy cure for skepticism. In my experience, unless the Lord intervenes in an extraordinary way, it takes a faithful follower of Jesus who is willing to commit to a long-term friendship and many honest conversations about the challenges they face and the changes the Lord has made in their own life. It is wonderful to see a hardened skeptic accept Jesus as his Savior and go on to a life of fruitfulness and blessing. It is exceedingly sad to see a hardened skeptic still clinging to doubt on his deathbed. Friendship with a determined skeptic is one of God's difficult assignments, but He will give you the strength and wisdom you need to see it through.

Another crutch that skeptics lean on is the claim of hypocrisy in the church. Of course there are hypocrites in the church! The church is not a place for perfect people; it is a place for broken, imperfect people. All of us are works in progress, and we need the Lord's grace and forgiveness on a daily basis. If someone says, "Well, the church is full of hypocrites," your reply should be, "You're right. Come on in. We'll move over and make room for one more!"

Life Trauma

All of us will face trauma at some point in our lives. For some of us, however, the trauma was so devastating that one or more aspects of our development came to a grinding halt. In some cases, such as abuse, this can result in a serious psychological condition that needs professional intervention. More often, I meet people who were traumatized by divorce or the death of a child or some injustice that was visited on them. For whatever reason, they were unable to process the legitimate emotions that tragedy brought on and move ahead.

This has spiritual consequences, too, when they are unable to accept that a loving God could allow such a thing to happen. They are convinced that God is not for them, but against them. Sometimes this can be worked through with the help of a wise and caring friend, but sometimes it requires the help of a trained counselor. If you are in a deep emotional valley like that, I encourage you to seek help. And if you have spiritual gifts that enable you to be that wise and caring friend, I hope you will allow yourself to be used by God in the lives of hurting people.

Cultural Differences

The body of Christ comprises people from every race, nation, language, and tribe. It's the original multicultural organization. Some of the most inspiring and humbling experiences I've ever had have been in worship with people who didn't look or sound like me. When you are surrounded by a group of people singing "Amazing grace! How sweet the sound that saved a wretch like me!" in a language other than your own, you will be reminded of just how diverse God's people are and of the vastness of His kingdom.

It is easy to become culturally biased and think that the gospel is for people who look and talk and live like we do. Nothing could be further from the truth. The gospel is for everyone, and it transcends every barrier that humans can construct to divide ourselves from each other. If you have the opportunity to share the love of Jesus with someone

> The gospel is for everyone, and it transcends every barrier that humans can construct to divide ourselves from each other.

from another culture or ethnicity or language group, I encourage you to put aside any awkwardness you may feel and do it. The Lord will honor your step of faith.

MAKING A DIFFERENCE IN YOUR NEIGHBORHOOD

We've discussed some of the obstacles we will face as we reach out to our neighbors. Now let's talk about how we can shine a light for the Lord down our streets, in our neighborhoods, and throughout our communities.

Be Salt and Light

I have heard something like this many times, and you have too: "I just don't want to put myself out there." But Jesus' consistent message was that we are to make advancing His kingdom our first priority. And He didn't make any exceptions, did He? He never said, "I don't expect to be the first priority for the busy ones, or the shy ones, or the ones who want to limit their faith to certain times and places and people."

On one occasion He told the crowd, "You are the salt of the earth. But if the salt loses its saltiness, how can it be made salty again? It is no longer good for anything, except to be thrown out and trampled underfoot." He also said, "You are the light of the world. A town built on a hill cannot be hidden. Neither do people light a lamp and put it under a bowl. Instead they put it on its stand, and it gives light to everyone in the house. In the same way, let your light shine before others, that they may see your good deeds and glorify your Father in heaven" (Matthew 5:13–16).

These were word pictures that Jesus' first-century listeners could relate to, and they still speak to us today. The Morton Salt Company notes that the first written reference to salt is found in the book of Job, one of the earliest books of the Bible, and that there are more than thirty other references to salt in the Scriptures.[1] Salt comes in much fancier containers these days, but its effect has not changed: it still preserves and seasons what it touches. Jesus is asking you to be like salt. He wants you to speak up and make a difference for Him and His values wherever you are—around your kitchen table, in your front yard, at your neighborhood playground, your grocery story, your workplace, your school board meetings, and all the other places where conversations shape beliefs and outcomes.

We're also called to be a light in the darkness. Did you know that you can see a tiny light from a great distance? Two astronomers measured the brightness of a single candle in complete darkness, and they discovered that the average unaided eye can see one small flame from 1.6 miles away![2]

You may have participated in a candlelight service where one person's candle lit another and another until the dark room became aglow with light. Don't think that your small efforts on behalf of God and His kingdom don't matter—they do! The darker the place you are in, the more brightly you will shine when you speak up for the Lord. And when your gospel flame spreads from one person to the next and the next, you will eventually look around and see that you have made a tremendous difference.

No matter how dire the circumstances around you seem, remember that Jesus is the hope the world needs, the light in the darkness that we have to share! He said, "I am the light of the world. Whoever follows me will never walk in darkness, but will have the light of life" (John 8:12). We live in a highly polarized season, but we are not called to huddle in our church buildings. We are called to stand boldly and proclaim the good news that Jesus is the Savior!

We've been sent to tell our neighbors that Jesus is for them, that He wants to have a relationship with them, that He offers them hope when everything else around them is in confusion and chaos. This is not just the responsibility of your pastor, or an evangelist, or some person who has a public platform. This is the calling and the assignment of the church—and that means every one of us.

I think one of the reasons God sent us home with the threat of millions of us dying is that we had lost any sense of mission—there was no purpose to our faith. We had perverted it into theological conversations that made us feel wise, and religious experiences that were focused on traditions and our own needs and desires.

Do you think that might describe you? Are you willing to lay your religious routine aside and discover God's purposes for your days under the sun? If you are, I encourage you to begin by cultivating an awareness of how God wants you to live. Say, "God, show me how to live with purpose for Your kingdom. Show me how to be Your advocate wherever I am. Show me how to live out the biblical perspective that I say I believe." This is a prayer that God loves to hear—and answer!

Tell Your Jesus-Story

I talk to people all the time who wonder if their Jesus-story is worth telling. I have a couple of thoughts on that. First, yes! And second, yes! Your story doesn't have to be filled with drama and miracles; the fact that God loves you and sent His Son to die in your place is the greatest miracle you will ever experience! Just tell about the reality of your walk with Jesus in your own words, and that will be enough.

Many years ago, we were trying to get electricity in a barn on our church property, but we kept bumping into bureaucratic roadblocks. I finally phoned the man who had the authority to run the power line. I described the situation, and he said, "That will never happen." "Why?" I asked. "Because barns don't have electricity," he replied matter-of-factly.

My dad was a veterinarian, and I grew up in the barns of Middle Tennessee. I began to list all of the barns I had personally been in where there was electricity, in my county and the surrounding counties. I wasn't asking for his opinion or approval; I was sharing the reality of what I had experienced. There was nothing he could say to deny that my experiences were real, and we eventually got power in the barn.

Your Jesus-story is what you know. It is your story of what you have seen Him do in your life, and no one can deny it. After Jesus healed a man, He told him, "Return home and tell how much God has done for you" (Luke 8:39). And that's all He's asking of you and me—to go to the people we know and tell them what God has done for us.

I often hear, "But Pastor, I don't speak well. I'm not very good with words." That's all right. Let everything else about your life—the actions of your life—speak so loudly that they can hear what you're not saying. And as I've seen time and again, the same God that loosened the tongue of Balaam's donkey (Numbers 22) can loosen the tongue of the most hesitant speaker.

I've known quiet people whose soft-spoken testimonies of what the Lord had done opened spiritual doorways that had been firmly closed for many years. As Peter said, "Worship Christ as Lord of your life. And if someone asks about your hope as a believer, always be ready to explain it" (1 Peter 3:15 NLT). I believe that if you are willing, the Holy Spirit will open your mouth and give you the words you need in every situation!

No Christian is flawless, and you need to be truthful about that. Have the courage to say, "My story isn't perfect. I have plenty of rough spots, but God is changing me. I'm a work in progress, but I want to honor the Lord with my life. My goal is to live with more integrity and grow closer to the Lord every day. Those things matter to me now. I don't always get it right, but following Jesus has made a big difference in my life. He has given me meaning and purpose, and my days are about more than impressing people and accumulating things. I'm excited to see what He will do with my life."

And you don't have to be in a church building to give someone an opportunity to profess their faith in Jesus. God has called me to be a pastor, and I have the privilege of extending those invitations from a stage. But you'd be surprised at how many opportunities present themselves at other times and places too—lifting weights at the gym, pondering the selection of ice cream at the grocery store, or sitting in a waiting room.

You can tell someone about Jesus wherever you are. If you will ask the Holy Spirit to give you opportunities to talk about your relationship with the Lord, He will honor that request. At first you may be surprised at how many people are open to hearing your Jesus-story and professing their faith in Him. Soon you will expect those God-moments because they will happen again and again. Day after day, wherever you are, never stop telling people about what the Lord has done for you and asking if they'd like to know Jesus too.

Let's Pray!

One of our ongoing emphases at World Outreach Church is learning to pray outside the walls of the church building and outside the safe atmosphere of our small groups. To help accomplish that, we began the Let's Pray! Initiative. I can say without hesitation that it has done a great deal to transform our congregation and has reached beyond our people and into our community. I want to encourage you to tap into the power of prayer and take it with you wherever you go. So let me tell you a little about Let's Pray!—how it works and what the results have been.

Let's Pray! is based on the foundational belief that prayer matters because prayer works. God wants to have a relationship with each one of us, and prayer is one of the ways we allow that relationship to unfold. James 5:16 says that "the prayer of a righteous person is powerful and effective." When we pray, we open doors for God's opportunities. When we fail to pray, those doors remain closed. It's that simple.

You interact with people in various settings every day. You stand in line at the grocery store. You sit in the bleachers during soccer practice. You wait while your tires are being rotated. You commiserate with a neighbor about the moles tunneling across your lawns. In these ordinary, seemingly insignificant places, you can become a God-agent in a whole new way.

It starts with your willingness to show genuine interest in other people. Begin by asking something like, "How are you today?" or "How's your day going?" Sometimes people will look at you strangely. Sometimes they will say they are fine and walk away. But many people will be glad to tell you how they are feeling. "I'm exhausted," she might say. "My husband is out of town, and my kids are sick. I was out of everything and had to make a grocery run." There's your God-opportunity to say, "Let's pray. God, help my friend make it until her husband gets home. Amen." Or he might say, "I had a flat tire today, and a new one is going to be more expensive than I thought." That's your opportunity to say, "Let's pray. God, help my friend find the money to pay for a new tire. Amen."

And that's it. You only get a few words. No questions. No

quoting Scripture. No asking for a response. Just say your prayer and move on with the conversation.

Our church folks have been doing this for several years now, and here's what I've discovered. If you'll summon the energy to express a little interest and the courage to have that brief "Let's pray" moment, people will respond. If they know you and interact with you regularly, they will begin to identify you as someone who prays. Soon they will be showing up for more—more prayer and more spiritual conversations. If you have a "Let's pray" moment with another parent in the bleachers, I promise you that person will just happen to sit near you the next time they have a problem.

I was at the gym running on a treadmill, and a man brought his friend over. He said, "I know you pray. This man's got a problem. Would you pray for him?" I said, "Sure, let's pray." And I did exactly what I described. Well, somebody told somebody, and now I get interrupted at the gym quite often. I've been standing right in the middle of the equipment with people running and lifting and sweating all around me, and someone will come up and say, "Will you pray with me?" Once a woman got down on her face on the carpet in the middle of the floor. I wasn't going to be outdone, so I got down there too, and we had a "Let's pray" moment.

We're living in a season when we desperately need God's possibilities to be a part of our world. The needs in people's lives are incredible—the stresses they feel, the pressures they're under, the burdens they bear. We've got a God-assignment, and He will help us with it if we'll open our hearts and be willing to be advocates for Him. You want to be known as a person who will open the door of God's possibilities any time someone unlocks it. Let your neighbors know that you are a person who believes in the power of prayer. Let them know you are willing to open the door for God to come through and work in their lives too. Let them know that your first response to life's challenges is "Let's Pray!"

Be a Spiritual Hotspot

Have you ever needed to connect to the internet but found yourself in a technological desert? That's when you need a hot-spot, a device that allows you to connect to the internet, wherever you are. I think that Paul allowed himself to be used as a spiritual hotspot. He said, "You know that I have not hesitated to preach anything that would be helpful to you but have taught you publicly and from house to house. I have declared to both Jews and Greeks that they must turn to God in repentance and have faith in our Lord Jesus" (Acts 20:20–21).

Wherever Paul was—in a synagogue, a marketplace, a home, a jail, a courtroom, or on the street—he wanted to connect people to Jesus. Sometimes people welcomed him, but just as often they threw stones. Paul knew that every one of those people desperately needed a relationship with the Lord, whether they realized it or not, so he persevered. That's what I desire for the Jesus followers in this generation. Wherever we encounter people—at home, at work, at school, in a waiting room, at the gym, or chatting at the mailbox—I want them to know that we will help them make a connection with God.

Sometimes that will mean a listening ear and an invitation to attend your church. The majority of people who visit a church for the first time come because someone invited them personally. Sometimes that will mean prayer. Sometimes that will mean telling what Jesus has done for you. Whether publicly or house to house, let's allow ourselves to be used to demonstrate God's love and build up His kingdom.

Show Hospitality

I think that Christians undervalue the influence they can have through the simple act of hospitality. The Barna Group studied the characteristics of Christian households and found that believers who regularly open their homes to visitors "are more likely to forge deep, meaningful relationships both within and outside of their homes."[3]

Too often we allow our pride to get in the way of our hospitality. Welcoming people into your life and your home is not about you or your home being perfect. Years ago, I lived in a condominium that had a hole in the floor inside the front door. It took a long time to get it fixed, and for a while you could see all the way down to the dirt! Groups were meeting there two nights a week, so I'd always greet them with, "Step over the hole."

If I had waited until all my house problems were fixed, or until I could impress them with my decorating and cooking skills, it would have been a long wait. I assure you that hospitality is a matter of the heart. The finest food served on the most elegant table is a tasteless meal when there is no love in the room. But a bologna sandwich on a paper plate is a feast when it is served by someone who loves the Lord and wants to share that love with other people.

The design of many modern neighborhoods inhibits neighborliness. Many of us pull into our driveways, open the garage door with a click, then go into the house and stay there until we leave again the same way. If we do go outside, it's into a fenced backyard. When you are aware of this, you're able to do some things to counter it. Sit on your front porch instead of in your backyard. If space allows, put some lawn furniture or a swing in your front yard and start spending time there. Walk through your neighborhood in the afternoon when people are getting home from work. Be friendly. Speak to people. Invite them to join you on your front porch or at your kitchen table.

I encourage you to practice hospitality. Don't worry about "entertaining"—that's meant to impress, and that's not what we should be concerned about. People today are starved for friendship and community, and they will be drawn to you like a magnet if you will put forth a little effort and make yourself accessible. It will bring good things to your life and the lives of many others.

Serve Others . . . in Jesus' Name

Many years ago we asked ourselves, "Would there be a void in our community if our church wasn't here?" After a lot of soul-searching, we came to the conclusion that no, our broader community wouldn't really miss us if we closed up shop and went home. We decided that we wanted to be a vital part of the community, and we set about making some changes that impact us to this day.

We began hosting a fall festival that we call Hoedown, and it has grown until now thousands of families from our community attend every year. We put on a weeklong summer day camp for hundreds of fourth, fifth, and sixth graders. We offer a free gift-wrapping service at our local mall during the month of December. We host community blood drives and food drives and toy drives. We offer our buildings and facilities to be used by other groups. I don't say this to brag; I say this to illustrate that we make an intentional effort to be a part of our community.

And we do it all with the message that we love and serve others because God first loved us, and we share out of the provision that He has lavished on us.

I am constantly amazed when I hear about the effective ministries that Christians have begun, sometimes as an initiative of their church and sometimes on their own. Car repair for single mothers and widows. Quilts for babies in the NICU. Home improvement projects for people on fixed incomes. Transitional programs for people leaving incarceration. Housing for women and children escaping domestic violence. Childcare during GED classes. Tutoring in public schools. ESL classes for adults. Respite for caregivers. Clothes closets. Food pantries. Mobile medical and dental units. The list could go on and on.

I've been in ministry long enough to know that every person who gives of themselves in these endeavors would tell me that they are blessed beyond any blessing they give. After all, Paul knew from experience what he wrote to the Ephesians: "Serve wholeheartedly, as if you were serving the Lord, not people, because you know that the Lord will reward each one for whatever good they do" (Ephesians 6:7–8).

Our primary goal in all of these things is to share the love of Christ. There should be a discernible difference between the people of God and a community organization that does good deeds. We are not a civic club with a theological background. We are not a theological debate society with a community service component. We are children of the King, and together we comprise His church. Yes, I believe that there is a social component to the gospel. But if all we focus on is the social component and we don't focus on the power of God to change lives, we forfeit the unique role of the church.

The people of God, the church, are united under the headship of Jesus of Nazareth to be an expression of the power of God and the love of God in our world—a physical, human demonstration of His boundless concern and care for people. Through our fragile earthen vessels, His power is made evident, and we become the invitation system for anyone else who would like to know that story. Out of that will come good deeds, but it all begins with and is based on the transformation of a personal life.

I believe that the contemporary church needs greater clarity of thought and purpose on this. God is not content to allow us to wander in half-hearted, lukewarm ambivalence. He does not want churches that look like just another nonprofit organization. We—as individual believers, local congregations, and the global church—need a new determination to be identified with our Savior. We need a new boldness to stand for the truth of the gospel in ways we haven't had to stand in our lifetime.

And Do It All with Humility

Peter, who knew a thing or two about speaking and acting impulsively, shared these simple words: "All of you, be like-minded, be sympathetic, love one another, be compassionate and humble" (1 Peter 3:8). Like-minded, sympathetic, loving, compassionate, and humble—Peter had learned those lessons himself and wanted us to benefit from his hard-won experience. These are all qualities we should desire for ourselves, but in my mind, the last word in Peter's list comes first. We have to humble ourselves in order to put the needs and concerns of others ahead of our own.

That's a pretty tall order for many of us—and frankly, a tall order for me. I have been fortunate to learn some lessons about humility from my parents. Please allow me to share a little of their story and how it has helped shape my thinking about ministry.

George and Betty Jackson were a busy young couple who had been in church all of their lives. But neither of them had an authentic, personal relationship with Jesus until they had been married for a few years and had three young sons. When God miraculously healed my mother of what she had been told was terminal cancer, the change was more than physical. That life event set both of my parents on a spiritual journey that changed them in ways they could never have expected.

They became hungry to know God and determined to serve Him. With my father's busy veterinary practice based in our home and three small boys underfoot, they began a Bible study in our living room. They let it be known that everyone in our community was welcome—no matter their race, their income, their background, or their baggage.

In spite of everything that might be considered an obstacle, including a de-scented pet skunk that sometimes ambled down the hallway, that Bible study flourished. When it outgrew any available living room, they moved to a hotel meeting room and reluctantly accepted the label of church. When it outgrew the meeting room, the group put up a tent on recently purchased land—a church complete with Porta-Potties! The Bible study eventually organized as a church, and the church has been blessed beyond anything they could have imagined.

Many, many people have come alongside my parents during these years, and the church would not be what we are today without them. But the first seed planted was George and Betty Jackson's simple desire to help their neighbors, both spiritually and physically. They never intended to start a church. They had

WE ARE STRONGER TOGETHER

a practice to run and three boys to raise, after all. They just knew then, as they know now, that people matter to Jesus, so they should matter to us too.

That is a scriptural lesson that I not only heard taught but have seen demonstrated in my parents' faithfulness—day after day, year after year, decade after decade. Their desire to help people know God has never waned. In fact, I believe they are as passionate about their calling as they have ever been, and their commitment to helping people is an example to everyone who knows them, including me.

Being a neighbor isn't very hard. It doesn't require an advanced degree or a big bank account. It doesn't mean starting a church. It just means caring about people and letting them see that you care. It means living intentionally among your neighbors instead of hiding behind your drawn curtains. It means showing genuine interest. Being kind. Acknowledging the dignity of people who are God's creation, made in His image.

Sometimes being a neighbor means that you'll have a Let's Pray! moment or an opportunity to tell your Jesus-story, but sometimes you won't. Either way, you will have been like-minded, sympathetic, loving, compassionate, and humble. Maybe that's not such a tall order after all.

WHAT DOES A NEIGHBOR LOOK LIKE?

A neighbor looks like a person who

- prays, "God, give me an opportunity to speak up for You today";

- thinks, "That person doesn't look like me, but they are made in the image of God just like I am. They are worthy of my time and concern";
- asks, "How are you doing today?" and opens the door to God through prayer;
- says, "Let me tell you what Jesus has done for me";
- invites people to church;
- shares a meal;
- mows a yard;
- shows concern for people . . . and does it all in Jesus' name.

The possibilities for neighborly service in God's kingdom are truly endless. I hope that you will ask the Holy Spirit to show you how you can give of your time, talent, energy, and resources to demonstrate the love of God to your neighbors and in your community.

CHAPTER 10

STRENGTH, COURAGE, AND HOPE

So be strong and courageous,
all you who put your hope in the Lord!
—PSALM 31:24 NLT

G od frequently reminds us to be strong and courageous. I believe we can reach heaven without having a neatly formed systematic theology, but I doubt we will achieve that goal without strength and courage. Following God is not always a journey of comfort and ease. Life is more difficult than we would prefer. Faith does not remove the difficulties. Add to the inherent challenges of day-to-day living the fact that God provides discipline.

He loves us too much to leave us without correction. No wonder we are repeatedly told to be strong and courageous!

One of the most remarkable demonstrations of strength and courage expressed in hope is found in the people of Israel. I first traveled to the Middle East when I was a boy. Back then Israel was a developing country with limited resources. The roads were poor, the struggle for survival was apparent, and the country was surrounded by enemies.

Years later I studied at Hebrew University in Jerusalem. The nation had changed. Cities had grown, industry had emerged, Jewish immigrants had returned from around the world. Israel had established herself as a part of the Middle Eastern community but was still surrounded by enemies.

I now have the privilege of visiting Israel on a regular basis. It is vastly different from the place I visited as a boy. Desalination plants along the Mediterranean provide an abundance of water—a first in the history of Israel. Israeli technology impacts the world. Agricultural products and irrigation innovations are exported to many nations. Israel is one of the most prosperous nations in the world—and is still surrounded by enemies.

> Hope is not secured by ease and comfort but by the awareness that God—not the posturing of our adversaries—defines our future.

I have learned many lessons from my Israeli friends; chief among them is that strength, courage, and vigilance are necessary to flourish in the midst of a "rough neighborhood." Weakness and apathy lead to forfeiture of freedom and opportunity. Hope is not secured by ease and comfort but by the awareness that God—not the posturing of our adversaries—defines our future.

Israelis have remained hopeful in the midst of great stress and consistent conflict. I am challenged by their faith. Jeremiah is not some shadowy character from antiquity referenced in the Hebrew Bible; he is part of the family tree. When you walk the dusty streets of Jerusalem, you stand on the stories of Scripture. Herod's temple foundations, Hezekiah's wall, the pool of Siloam—all of these are tangible reminders that God has been keeping His promises for many centuries. They provide a living hope for the challenges of today.

Israel's enemies are persistent. Iran still boldly declares an intent to develop nuclear weapons and annihilate Israel. Only God can secure the future of the nation, but He will not do it apart from the people—He will do it through them. If you're unsure what the future holds for the nation of Israel, listen to God speaking through the prophet Amos:

> "New wine will drip from the mountains
> and flow from all the hills,
> and I will bring my people Israel back from exile.
> They will rebuild the ruined cities and live in
>   them.
> They will plant vineyards and drink their wine;
> they will make gardens and eat their fruit.
> I will plant Israel in their own land,
> never again to be uprooted
> from the land I have given them,"

> says the Lord your God. (Amos 9:13–15)

After almost two thousand years of exile, God is restoring the Jewish people to their ancient homeland in fulfillment of his promise to Abraham. Their young men and women serve in the military, the scientists work diligently to improve life in the desert, and technology has changed patterns of life. But I believe that God gave the knowledge and the insight to facilitate those breakthroughs. And I have to smile at the specificity of God. If you drive through Israel from the Golan Heights in the north to the Negev deserts in the south, you'll pass vineyard after vineyard. Quite literally, new wine is dripping from the landscape of Israel. God is faithful to His Word.

And if He's faithful to Israel, He'll be faithful to you and me.

GOD IS PURIFYING HIS CHURCH

Just as God is regathering the Jewish people, He is purifying His church. Perhaps the most precipitous decline in the influence of Christianity in America has happened during my lifetime. Historically, the most damaging things you can do to the church are to leave it in peace and make it affluent. And both those things happened in abundance following World War II. Yes, there have been conflicts that affected Americans, but they did not have much negative effect on the American church.

Before the COVID-19 pandemic struck our world, the church had become pretty complacent. Generally speaking, we were more concerned about going along and fitting in. Standing out from the crowd for any reason other than success and acclaim were not our priorities. Most of the conversation among theological academics and prominent pastors was about building bridges to our culture and making sure everyone felt loved. Tolerance and inclusivity and the other buzzwords that drive much of the cultural dialogue drove the dialogue in the church as well.

The global pandemic has thrown down a spiritual gauntlet that is impossible to sidestep or ignore. We have been reminded that God is holy and righteous, and the church has the responsibility to be His ambassadors in the world. I think we are being reawakened to the fact that our most important assignment in the world is to pursue holiness and show the world what that looks like.

The Corinthian church struggled with many of the same problems that we do. They became believers in Jesus in the midst of a city where holiness was an unknown word. Corinth was a prosperous center of culture and trade, but it was also well known for its pagan temples to various gods. The holiness that Paul called these new believers to could not have been any further from the way they had been living.

He wrote to them,

> "Come out from them
> and be separate,
> says the Lord.
> Touch no unclean thing,
> and I will receive you."

And,

> "I will be a Father to you,
> and you will be my sons and daughters,
> says the Lord Almighty."

Therefore, since we have these promises, dear friends, let us purify ourselves from everything that contaminates body and spirit, perfecting holiness out of reverence for God. (2 Corinthians 6:17–7:1)

Paul sounded pretty adamant about what is required, didn't he? Come out. Be separate. Touch no unclean thing. Purify yourself. Perfect holiness. Paul wanted us to understand that God expects us to be different from the world around us. We shouldn't be asking, "How far is too far? How close is too close? How much is too much?" Instead, we should be pursuing holiness with our every thought and breath.

When I say that God is purifying His church, I mean that God is purifying you and me. He doesn't want us to do anything that diminishes our godliness and holiness. He doesn't want us to go anywhere, watch anything, listen to anything, or touch anything that would diminish our godliness and holiness.

What is God's promise to us when we pursue Him with our whole selves? He will be a Father to us, and we will be His sons and daughters. I encourage you to make this your life's ambition. We are not promised a long life, and even the longest life is but a blink of an eye in light of eternity. Choose godliness, and then be prepared to share the story of your transformation with everyone who asks about the changes they see in you.

I assure you, strength and courage will be demanded as you pursue God. Our hope is secure by the faithfulness of His promises. Governments, economies, investments, and even friends may bring disappointment, but God's faithfulness secures our future.

REASONS FOR HOPE

Discipline does not mean we have been abandoned. In Hebrews we are reminded that God disciplines all His children. Discipline and maturing are seldom pleasant experiences, but they are necessary components to productive living. God disciplined the Jewish people, and He is disciplining His church. If we will be trained by the expression of His love, we will receive the fulfillment of His promises.

God's love secures our future. One of the remarkable assertions of Scripture is that God loves people. No explanation is offered, just the blunt and persistent expression of God's love. We are often rebellious, ungodly, ungrateful, and determined to walk away—yet God's love persists. He cares for each of us. He knows the worst part of our stories and the darkest part of our thoughts, and He still cares for us.

> If we will be trained by the expression of His love, we will receive the fulfillment of His promises.

Through Jesus' redemptive work God has made provision that we can be forgiven, redeemed, and included in His kingdom. All of this is an expression of His love for us—never earned or deserved—an expression of God's compassion.

God is watching over all. That is not a threat, it is a tremendous promise! The psalmist wrote, "he who watches over you will not slumber; indeed, he who watches over Israel will neither slumber nor sleep" (Psalm 121:3–4). Rejection and abandonment are a part of our journey through time. But God does not abandon us. His constant watchful care is a force for our good. God has accepted us and welcomed us into the midst of His purposes. Remember what Moses told Joshua: "Be strong and courageous. Do not be afraid or terrified because of them, for the LORD your God goes with you; he will never leave you nor forsake you" (Deuteronomy 31:6).

God is purifying His church in the midst of the chaos of our world. Strength and courage will be required of each of us. Our hope is secured by God's faithfulness, not by the institutions of government or by pleasant circumstances. If God has disciplined you, cooperate with Him. Humble yourself and repent. If God is asking you to persevere through a difficult season, quietly thank Him for His faithfulness. Our future is secure. The one who promised is faithful. God is not intimidated by our circumstances or the threats of our adversaries. Our God is a deliverer!

CHAPTER 11

EYES ON THE PRIZE

> I focus on this one thing: Forgetting the past and looking forward to what lies ahead, I press on to reach the end of the race and receive the heavenly prize for which God, through Christ Jesus, is calling us.
>
> —PHILIPPIANS 3:13-14 NLT

We're probably all a little motivated by the thought of winning a prize. Prizes start early in life and come in many forms: a gold star on a chore chart, a medal for the potato sack race on Field Day, a blue ribbon for an apple pie at the county fair, a certificate for surpassing our sales goals. But Paul had a different kind of prize in his sights. This is actually a biblical principle, not just an instant insight from the apostle Paul: forgetting the past and focusing on what God is doing is essential to sustaining faith under pressure. The Bible and church history are full of examples

> Forgetting the past and focusing on what God is doing is essential to sustaining faith under pressure.

of people who refused to succumb to disappointment and discouragement and chose instead to remain laser focused on God's faithfulness.

Paul certainly had accomplished a great deal at this point in his life. He had received a good education. He had left behind a promising career with the Pharisees to accept Jesus' invitation to follow and serve Him. After he met Jesus and began advocating for Him, he preached whenever there was an opportunity, launched churches, mentored leaders, and wrote letters that have impacted people for two thousand years.

Let's take a look at a few biblical examples of people who had their eyes set on eternity, starting with Paul himself.

PAUL: "I PRESS ON"

As we discussed in chapter 3, Paul was probably the most influential ambassador for Christ the world has ever known. But his ministry years were incredibly challenging, both mentally and physically, and many of the later ones were spent in prison. Think about what he wrote to the Corinthian church:

Five times I received from the Jews the forty lashes minus one. Three times I was beaten with rods, once I was pelted with stones, three times I was shipwrecked, I spent a night and a day in the open sea, I have been constantly on the move. I have

been in danger from rivers, in danger from bandits, in danger
from my fellow Jews, in danger from Gentiles; in danger in the
city, in danger in the country, in danger at sea; and in danger
from false believers. (2 Corinthians 11:24–26)

Paul casually mentioned that once he had been "pelted with
stones," and this may be the occasion described in Acts 14:19
when he was stoned until his attackers left him for dead. Paul's
experience of serving the Lord was filled with hardships and even
danger, yet he never took his eyes off his goal. How was he able
to do that?

Paul Kept a Laser-Sharp Focus

I'll admit that it can be hard to stay focused on spiritual
things, and especially on a heavenly reward that might seem a
little hazy and far in the future. We are eternal creatures, and
we know that we can look forward to a glorious eternity. But for
now, we are participants in time, and much of our emotional
energy is invested in the day-to-day reality of what is happening here.

I have found that we often give less than our best to the
things of God. Instead, we give our greatest efforts and make
our most significant sacrifices for our children, our careers, our
sports teams, and our hobbies. For many of us it doesn't seem
strange to endure blazing heat or freezing temperatures to see a
football game—and pay for the privilege to do so. How many of
us would endure that to hear God's Word preached? God actually
reprimanded a group of priests who were casually offering Him
blemished animal sacrifices. He wanted them to know that He
had noticed their indifference toward Him. "When you bring

that kind of offering," He asked, "why should [I] show you any favor at all?" (Malachi 1:9, author's paraphrase).

Paul seemed to have overcome much of that human tendency. Can you hear the intent, the purpose, in his letter to the Philippians? "I'm focused on one thing," he said. "I've left the past behind. I'm looking to the future. I press on!" And what was the prize he was so focused on? The reward he so earnestly sought to receive? "The heavenly prize for which God, through Christ Jesus, is calling us."

The consistent message of Scripture is to reassess our priorities, realign our calendars, get focused, harness our energies, and go to work for the Lord. I invite you to do what I do on a regular basis. First, look at your daily schedule, your monthly calendar, and your expenditures. Then think about where you are investing your time, your energies, and your resources. If you find significant gaps between your plans and purposes and God's plans and purposes, it's time for a reset.

Does your life demonstrate that you desire God's best enough to give Him your best? I want to be like Paul and have a laser-sharp focus on the Lord. I want to give Him my best, no matter what is going on around me. I want to give Him my whole heart with nothing held back. I want my motivation, and yours, to be the same as Paul's: to press on and finish well so that in due time we will receive that heavenly prize.

Paul Learned to Be Content

Paul had learned a lesson that would be helpful for each one of us: how to be content, no matter the circumstances we are in. "I am not saying this because I am in need, for I have learned to be content whatever the circumstances. I know what it is to be in need, and I know what it is to have plenty," he wrote to the believers in Philippi. "I have learned the secret of being content in any and every situation, whether well fed or hungry, whether living in plenty or in want" (Philippians 4:11–12).

Sometimes contentment can seem like an unattainable goal. We all know we should be content with what we have, but there are very few voices in our culture encouraging that attitude. The devil is a master of convincing us that we should never be content. And we are bombarded with messages that we will be happier and more successful if we pursue more things, newer things, and better things.

People's desire for material things is certainly nothing new. Ancient Egyptian royals are famous because they filled their tombs with things they thought they would need in eternity, but today those objects are nothing more than artifacts in museums. We have our own issues with things. We fill our homes with more than we need, then rent storage units to house the overflow. When we're gone, our relatives are left with things they never wanted. If they are not sold for pennies on the dollar, they will go to a thrift store or the trash heap. I have officiated at many funerals, and I have never seen a moving van following the hearse!

Much of this behavior results from peer pressure and a desire to keep up with our friends and neighbors. If keeping up with the Joneses has been a goal in your life, I encourage you to go outside and stand in your front yard right now. Wave a white flag and yell as loudly as you can, "They win! We surrender to the Joneses!" No matter how hard you try to keep up, someone else will always have a bigger television, a newer vehicle, a greener yard, and softer towels. As nice as those things are, they will not matter a bit in eternity.

Paul reminded Timothy of how pointless it is to worry about the things of this world, because they have no lasting value. Instead, he urged Timothy to concentrate on his standing with God: "But godliness with contentment is great gain. For we brought nothing into the world, and we can take nothing out of it. But if we have food and clothing, we will be content with that" (1 Timothy 6:6–8).

I urge you not to allow yourself to become overly concerned about material things. Instead, put your time and energy into your relationship with the Lord. When He becomes your first priority, your joy and happiness will increase and everything else will fall into place.

DANIEL: "LORD, LISTEN! LORD, FORGIVE! LORD, HEAR AND ACT!"

Paul was educated in the school of the respected Jewish teacher Gamaliel, and he would have known every detail of Daniel's story. Although Paul never quoted Daniel directly, his writings have echoes of the same devotion to God and perseverance in the face of great difficulties. Paul seemed to be comparing himself to Daniel in his second letter to Timothy: "But the Lord stood at my side and gave me strength, so that through me the message might be fully proclaimed and all the Gentiles might hear it. And I was delivered from the lion's mouth" (2 Timothy 4:17).

Daniel Was Undeterred

Daniel was a remarkable man of faith, and he is one of my heroes too. He had been enslaved since he was a young man and had every reason to be filled with bitterness, but he was not. We're not given much insight into that; we simply know that Daniel's greatest desire was to please the Lord.

Daniel is perhaps best known for surviving a brush with death in a lion's den. But the accounts of Daniel's relationship with God include many more demonstrations of Daniel's loyalty and God's deliverance and blessing. He was so devoted to God that he kept praying, even knowing that he would be executed for it (Daniel 6). God dispatched an angel to him—twice—to tell him that he was highly esteemed, and his prayers were immediately acted on. "As soon as you began to pray, a word went out, which I have come to tell you, for you are highly esteemed," Gabriel told him in Daniel 9:23.

Daniel Was Humble

Daniel's prayer in chapter 9 humbles and motivates me: "Lord, the great and awesome God, who keeps his covenant of love with those who love him and keep his commandments, we have sinned and done wrong. We have been wicked and have rebelled; we have turned away from your commands and laws. . . . We do not make requests of you because we are righteous, but because of your great mercy. Lord, listen! Lord, forgive! Lord, hear and act!" (vv. 4–5, 18–19).

Daniel was a man of constant prayer and was highly esteemed by God, yet here he prayed as if he were among the most wicked of people. Instead of pointing his finger at all the evildoers around him, verse 3 says that Daniel "turned to the Lord God and pleaded with him in prayer and petition, in fasting, and in sackcloth and ashes."

What if Daniel had set his mind on other things? What if he

had been angry and defiant toward God over his enslavement and mistreatment? What if he had not bothered to pray? Daniel's perspective was not limited to his earthly existence; if that had been his only vantage point, he would have forfeited the opportunities God placed before him. He refused to let the immediacy of his circumstances deter him from honoring God because his life was fueled by a view beyond time.

Do we approach God with anywhere near that same kind of humility and desperation? Our world is shaking at its very foundation, yet we have separated ourselves from what is happening as if it has nothing to do with us. We act as if we had no part in getting us to this place and no belief that God can impact our future for the better. The problem in our world is not the depravity of the wicked. It's the indifference in the hearts of the faithful.

> The problem in our world is not the depravity of the wicked. It's the indifference in the hearts of the faithful.

Do you believe God can change the course of history? I do! I'm not filled with despair when I look at what's happening around me. I'm filled with the desire to pray. In order for us to live with Daniel's kind of perspective, we have to lift our eyes above the horizon and have a hope, a faith, and a confidence in a future that extends beyond what is reported to us by the news. We have to dream differently than the people who haven't put their faith in a living God.

This is our time in the arena, and our chapter of history is being written. It is time for us to get on our knees, humble ourselves, and seek the Lord's forgiveness. Our distinctiveness is not that we sit for a few minutes in a church building. Our distinctiveness is that we have a hope that reaches beyond time.

It is time for us to tell the world that a relationship with almighty God is important. It is time for us to act like Jesus really does make a difference in our lives—in our conversations, in our marriages, in our parenting, in our work, in our recreation, and in every other part of our lives.

JESUS...AND ONLY JESUS

Jesus' uniqueness and authority have been challenged since the earliest days of His ministry. The scenes and the methods have changed, but the pressure put on His followers to say that He is not the only Son of God, the Messiah, has not.

The Roman Pantheon

The Pantheon is one of many magnificent Roman buildings that survive from antiquity. Construction began in 27 BC. Its walls are twenty feet thick, and its bronze doors are twenty-seven feet high. The dome was the largest built at that time, and its exact method of construction has never been determined.[1]

The interior is exquisitely beautiful because it was built to house statues of their gods. Each time the Romans conquered a new people, the god of that group was placed in a niche in the wall. The vanquished people didn't have to reject their faith and stop worshiping their own god; they just had to acknowledge the deity of the ever-expanding group of gods and the worldviews they represented. It was the public policy of the day, a religious compromise to keep people content enough that they would not revolt.

The Roman emperor was regarded as a god, and anyone who dared to claim otherwise was in direct opposition to the power of the empire. The Roman authorities began to put real pressure on the Christians to worship him, but those early believers had both conviction and courage. When the Romans accused, "You don't believe in the gods of Rome," they responded, "No, we don't. With all your gods, you don't truly have one. Jesus is not just another god; He is the one and only God. And Christianity is not just one more religious option among many."

Those Christians understood that asserting this about Jesus threatened not just their livelihoods but their very lives; yet they persevered. If the early Christians had succumbed to the pressure of the authorities that ruled over them, we would not be worshiping on Sundays.

The Price of Compromise

The word for the Romans' method of religious blending is *syncretism*. And before you think, "How ridiculous!" understand that syncretism is very popular among those of us who sit in churches today. We identify as Christian, but we incorporate pagan worldviews with those beliefs.

There are many congregations where you can discuss the validity of the teachings of Muhammad along with the teachings of Jesus. Others have incorporated Eastern philosophies into their faith and practice, including yoga and meditation. Many have legitimized unbiblical ideas of sexuality, marriage, and family. Some have adopted a social justice gospel or an environmental gospel or an economic gospel. All this is happening while they are reluctant to assert that Jesus is the way, the truth, and the life.

Make no mistake about this: the gospel is centered in a life reconciled to God through faith in Jesus Christ. That's the message the church has for the world. And if we reprioritize the gospel to put other things before that, our message is compromised and weakened.

The best outcomes for humanity happen when we focus on the fundamentals of our faith and allow the Holy Spirit to transform our character from the inside out. Only then will we treat one another with respect and dignity. Only then will we behave in ways that create and support godly communities and, in turn, a godly nation.

I believe that syncretism and the compromise that results is one of the reasons God is shaking the church. This is not some distant, theoretical discussion. The conflict is present today, and it will only intensify in the days ahead. We've been reluctant to address it because we have been timid, or distracted, or disinterested, or perhaps uncertain. But we can no longer sit by in silence.

We simply cannot say that Jesus is just another option for belief. We cannot continue to open our church buildings to unbiblical practices. We cannot say that the Bible is just another book of stories to be interpreted as we please. We must tell the world that Jesus is the only Son of God, and He gave Himself so that all humanity might know the Father. We must protect the church from indifference and be careful about what is said and done under our auspices and in our facilities. We must state without hesitation that God's Word is His gift to us and our guide for life.

Are you willing to examine your beliefs and your behaviors

and align them with the truth that you know? If you are willing to commit yourself to a new standard of holiness and purity regarding your beliefs and your actions, please say this prayer with me:

Heavenly Father, I pause to repent. To repent of my willful disobedience to You and my stubborn refusal to acknowledge my own ungodly choices, even when I knew what You had asked of me. I repent of suppressing the truth and refusing to speak when I knew the truth. I turn away from all ungodliness, and I choose a new path of thought and action. I choose to be pleasing in Your sight. Look on me with mercy and kindness and not with anger. In Jesus' name, amen.

The Suffering Church

The people of God have often been pressured to revise or recant their belief in Jesus. When we first meet the apostle Paul, he is Saul of Tarsus, a murderer and blasphemer whose goal was to discredit Jesus' followers and destroy the church. Roman emperors sometimes illuminated their garden parties with Christians dipped in tar and set afire. Hitler's Third Reich imprisoned and eventually executed Dietrich Bonhoeffer, a pastor and theologian who had joined the German military intelligence agency in order to work undercover in the resistance movement.[2] From prison he wrote, "The great masquerade of evil has played havoc with all our ethical concepts. For evil to appear disguised as light, charity, historical necessity, or social justice is quite bewildering to anyone brought up on our traditional ethical concepts, while for the Christian who bases his life on the Bible, it merely confirms the fundamental wickedness of evil."[3] In many countries of the world, house churches meet in secret while other believers choose to worship openly, knowing that their lives are in danger because of it.

I've encountered some believers who have adopted the idea that the church will never have to suffer. That's a very difficult perspective to share if you know the history of the church or have even a modest knowledge of the church in the world today. To visit the Christians in Afghanistan, China, Russia, Iran, Iraq, Somalia, or dozens of other places that we could name and tell them they will never have to suffer for their faith reflects a staggering lack of awareness and sensitivity.

The truth is that it is very difficult to be a Christian in many places in the world. There are not many voices advocating for Jesus' persecuted followers, because those of us who have freedom and liberty to worship God are either unaware of what they are going through or unconcerned because it doesn't seem to affect us. I believe that someday we will be called to account for our lack of concern and action on their behalf.

Here are the haunting words of Martin Niemöller, a German pastor who acknowledged his own anti-Semitism and the complicity of Protestant church leaders in the Holocaust:

> First they came for the socialists, and I did not
>> speak out—
>> because I was not a socialist.
> Then they came for the trade unionists, and I did
>> not speak out—
>> because I was not a trade unionist.
> Then they came for the Jews, and I did not
>> speak out—

because I was not a Jew.

Then they came for me—

and there was no one left to speak for me.[4]

I am inspired by the stories of God's people living faithfully through the ages, even in the face of great persecution and possible death. It once seemed that persecution for our faith would be impossible in America; today I am not so sure. I have hope for the church in this season, however, because I see God's people gathering together and demonstrating faithfulness, courage, and confidence that I haven't seen before.

In order to live with the certainty of God's faithfulness and experience His peace and joy through discouraging times, we must continually evaluate where our focus is. We need to stay aware of the world we're in, but we don't want to be so immersed in it that we cannot see God.

Remember that our future is not secured by the stock market or the prevailing ideology of the day or any group of politicians. Our future is anchored by our King and our trust in Him. So when you see discouraging things happening around you, stop and thank the Lord that His kingdom will endure forever. He is secure, and He has secured the final victory for us.

Empires rise and fall, and the social context changes, but the church of Jesus Christ continues forward. Think of the empires that have come and gone while the church has spread throughout the earth. Whether on a riverbank, or in a house, a prison cell, a tent, or a beautiful building, the message of redemption through Jesus Christ is shared, and believed, and the church continues to grow.

Every believer in Jesus of Nazareth carries the same

assignment, no matter the generation, no matter the context. So no matter what comes, I want to be known as a person who lived faithfully during my days on the earth. I want to be known as a person who kept my eyes on the prize. And I pray that for you as well.

TRUE FREEDOM AND LIBERTY

It has become common to see people demonstrating or marching for freedom and liberty. They usually are looking for some action from the government that will free them from some oppression or mistreatment. But true freedom and liberty for all will not come from a government or an ideology or a political party. True freedom will come only when the church has the courage to say that Jesus will bring freedom and liberty, because only He can transform the hearts of people.

Paul knew true freedom, even as he wrote from a prison cell: "Where the Spirit of the Lord is, there is freedom" (2 Corinthians 3:17). Jesus laid down His life to purchase our freedom, and the Holy Spirit invites us to a similar behavior. Not to arrogance, not to pride, not to selfish ambition, not to the pursuit of pleasure, but to lay down our lives in humility and serve Him.

My prayer for us is that we will stop pointing fingers and fall to our knees. My prayer is that we will examine our hearts to see where we are falling short in loyalty and service to our King. My prayer is that we will invite Jesus to be more than a Savior to us; I pray that we will invite Him to be Lord. Lord of our hearts. Lord of our hands. Lord of our thoughts. Lord of our words. Lord of our homes. Lord of our resources.

Have you asked Jesus to be your Savior but held back parts of yourself from His lordship? Ask the Holy Spirit to show you how to make Jesus Lord of all. Ask Him to help you keep your eyes on the prize. These are requests that He is happy to hear and happy to answer.

THE REWARDS ARE REAL

The rewards we receive for faithfully following Jesus are both temporal and eternal, in this life and the next. Jesus explained in Matthew 16:24–27 that what we do to receive rewards in His kingdom is counterintuitive, but nevertheless, it is what He expects us to do.

> Then Jesus said to his disciples, "Whoever wants to be my disciple must deny themselves and take up their cross and follow me. For whoever wants to save their life will lose it, but whoever loses their life for me will find it. What good will it be for someone to gain the whole world, yet forfeit their soul? Or what can anyone give in exchange for their soul? For the Son of Man is going to come in his Father's glory with his angels, and then he will reward each person according to what they have done."

The writer of Hebrews had this perspective on Jesus' life, both in time and in eternity: "Fixing our eyes on Jesus, the pioneer and perfecter of faith. For the joy set before him he endured the cross, scorning its shame, and sat down at the right hand of the throne of God" (Hebrews 12:2).

We might think of time and eternity as two separate things,

but they are in fact a seamless whole. In time, Jesus was nailed to a Roman cross and left to suffocate. He was publicly humiliated and died alongside two criminals. Jesus endured that because of the joy that was set before Him. The joy wasn't in time, because Jesus was never vindicated before His enemies. As far as they were concerned, He was dead and out of their way. But Jesus endured so that He could take His place at God's right hand in eternity.

History shows and we can observe that denying yourself and following Jesus is simply the best way to live. It will bring you joy that results from living within His plans and purposes. It will bring you happiness that is beyond anything the world has to offer. The joy and happiness that come from following Jesus are contagious. The people around you will see that you are different, that you are living for something greater than yourself, and they will want that too.

When Jesus returns, He will reward each person according to what he or she has done during their days on the earth. And those rewards will stretch into eternity. I've concluded that God isn't going to reward me for what this world might see as my successes and achievements, because God doesn't need those things. If I accumulate a billion dollars, God doesn't breathe a sigh of relief and say, "That's good. The tithe of that will fund My next initiative." If I earn multiple degrees, the hosts of heaven don't say, "Okay, we can relax. Allen has the answers we need."

It isn't my success or my achievements that matter for eternity; it is my faithfulness. Every one of us can be faithful, regardless of how the world sees the circumstances of our lives. And when we choose to be faithful, God will respond to that with blessings and rewards in this life and the next.

I urge you to be like Paul and keep your eyes on the prize,

> It isn't my success or my achievements that matter for eternity; it is my faithfulness.

no matter your circumstances. If you don't believe there's a reward, you'll fold like a cheap tent when challenges come—and so will I. But if you believe that God will reward you in eternity for the way you yielded to Him and served Him in time, you'll be able to persevere when difficult seasons come. It will give your life purpose and meaning that no set of career objectives can. And it is one goal that you will never regret. The following is "A Proclamation of Faith" that we've adopted here at World Outreach Church. I hope it's an encouragement to you:

God has uniquely blessed us—the best is yet to come.

The earth is the Lord's and everything in it.

He is the sovereign creator of all things.

Nothing is too difficult for Him, His love sustains us.

Jesus, His only Son, is our Savior, Lord & King.

We live in a season of shaking. God is shaking the earth.

He is restoring the Jewish people and purifying His church.

If we look at the things which can be shaken we will be filled with terror.

If we look at the eternal Kingdom of our Lord, we will be filled with anticipation.

Our determination is to declare before one another & Almighty God

WE WILL NOT STOP.

CHAPTER 12

STAND AND BE COUNTED

A final word: Be strong in the Lord and in his mighty power. Put on all of God's armor so that you will be able to stand firm against all strategies of the devil. For we are not fighting against flesh-and-blood enemies, but against evil rulers and authorities of the unseen world, against mighty powers in this dark world, and against evil spirits in the heavenly places.
—EPHESIANS 6:10–12 NLT

Several years ago, our church held a men's event in the local university's football stadium. It was a hot summer night, so most of us were in shorts and T-shirts. One guy who had played football there wore his jersey for old times' sake.

We began the evening with everyone sitting in the bleachers, but near the end of the program, we asked every man to get up from his seat and walk onto the field. Something so remarkable happened that I remember it like it was yesterday. Chatter turned to silence as men began to realize that they were no longer in the place where people sit and watch; they were in the place where battles are fought.

Unless you've played a sport under big-time stadium lights, you don't realize the difference between the lighting in the bleachers and on the field. The lighting in the bleachers is bright enough to see your popcorn, but that is nothing compared to the intensity of the lighting that is focused on the players.

And the man who had worn his jersey looked a lot more prepared than the rest of us. We looked like we were there to have a good time. He looked like a man who had come ready to defend his territory. Even the feel of the turf underneath us was a reminder that this was no playground; this was a place where you would need shoes with cleats in order to stay on your feet when the shoving started.

There was no football on the field, no crowd in the stands, and no band playing. But the glare of the lights and the feel of the turf seemed to take everyone to a different place. I talked to many of those men later, and our reactions were similar. Each one of us felt a little inadequate on that field. Each one of us realized that there is an enormous difference between being a spectator and being a participant.

We have imagined that following Christ means being a casual observer who watches from the bleachers. We have been content to allow other people to summon their courage, take risks, and live out their faith. But the strength of God's church is not fully expressed when God's people stay in the comfort and safety of their seats. It is fully expressed when we accept our role as spiritual leaders who are willing to bring godly influence to bear in our homes, workplaces, and communities. It is when we take hold of the courage Jesus gives us, then stand up and walk onto the field to engage the battle for righteousness alongside our Lord and King.

BE COURAGEOUS

It is very difficult to know how to respond when we are challenged by things we can't see. We can't place fear under a microscope. We can't put confusion in a test tube. We can't hold panic in our hands. It is easy to be shackled by those things during a season of unrest. But if you know Jesus, those things do not have to be your response, no matter what you are facing.

Jesus faced many difficult situations that we might think would cause Him to be afraid, confused, or panicked—but He never lost trust. Courage is not the absence of fear; I believe you can do courageous things while battling fear. Trust is the antidote to fear; trust fuels courage. Jesus knew that His Father had a purpose and a plan for His days on the earth, and He fully trusted Him to complete them. That knowledge and His faith in His Father enabled Him to react with calm assurance to whatever the Enemy sent His way.

> **Trust is the antidote to fear; trust fuels courage.**

Jesus told His disciples, "Take courage! It is I. Don't be afraid" (Matthew 14:27). This is an assertive statement. It tells me that Jesus wants me to avoid passively allowing my heart and mind to be filled with the confusion and chaos that make up most of the news cycle and create panic and fear. Instead, I should be proactive and fill my mind with God's Word. I should remind myself of His loving care and surround myself with voices who speak His truth.

The battle is indeed the Lord's, and we will need His help to win it, so grab on to the courage He promises and do not let go. Remember that God has a purpose and a plan for you, and you can trust Him to see you through!

BE READY TO LEAD

I have never seen a greater need for Christians who are ready to step up and provide leadership in every part of our culture. I used to think that leadership was mainly a concern of the secular world and that I was too spiritual to give it much thought. Then God awakened me to the reality that for Christians, leadership is just another way of describing the action of standing up for Him and influencing the world. That is a big part of the church's assignment, which means it is my assignment and your assignment.

We think of leadership as coming from the top down, but leadership is not just about a title or a position on an organizational chart. You may have a title or a position, but as John Maxwell says, "He that thinketh he leadeth, and hath no one following, is only taking a walk."[1]

Real leadership is about having real influence. When Jesus said, "You are the salt of the earth. . . . You are the light of the world" (Matthew 5:13–14), He simply meant that we are here to make a difference for Him. If the Holy Spirit asks you to run for office or assume a public leadership role, I hope you will do that. But leadership begins in the places where we are and with the people who are already within our reach: our homes and families, our workplaces and coworkers, our communities and our neighbors. These are the places and people that must change before we will see significant change on a bigger stage, so we must approach all of these assignments with a biblical perspective.

I know Christians whose "day jobs" require great leadership skills. They run a business, teach a classroom, oversee a factory floor, argue for a client in court, or save a life in an operating room. But when it comes to bringing their faith into that context, they say, "I'm not qualified to do that" or "I don't want to impose my personal beliefs on those people." The theological word for that attitude is *Baloney!* We are not called to sit on the sidelines and wait for someone else to come along and change the world for God.

Some people think, "That's what I pay the preacher to do!" Your pastor and the other staff at your church have their own kingdom assignments, but you do too. There is nothing in Scripture that says their calling and their responsibilities diminish your calling and your responsibilities. Every one of us is called to be a voice for Jesus wherever we are.

BE READY TO SHARE YOUR JESUS-STORY

Samuel Shoemaker was a fascinating man who served as the rector of Calvary Episcopal Church in New York City from 1925 to 1952. He was influenced by a wide range of faith leaders and was devoted to discipleship, personal evangelism, and missionary work. His church operated the rescue mission where Bill Wilson, the founder of Alcoholics Anonymous, began his meetings, and his spiritual guidance influenced that program.

What is even more interesting about Sam Shoemaker is his conviction that the gospel should be spread primarily through "lay witnesses." He founded the Faith at Work initiative that began with group meetings and spread to include conferences, a magazine, and a radio show.

One man who shared his conviction about sharing your faith at work was his church's janitor. The janitor told a painter about Jesus, and they began meeting in the boiler room of the church building. A baggage handler from Grand Central Station, Ralston Young, Red Cap #42, started meeting with them. He began telling people about Jesus as he carried their bags and eventually began holding prayer meetings in an empty train car at the station.[2] None of those men sat at the top of their company's organizational chart. But they had influence in their world, and they used it to introduce people to Jesus.

God can use people where they are or move people to where He wants them. Both Joseph and Daniel were sold into slavery in foreign lands, but they used their influence for God even in that context. The apostle Paul had pursued influence in one world, but God picked him up and drop-kicked him into another world where his influence would be even greater. Did you know that you, too, are a person of influence? You can be on the top line of an organizational chart or the bottom. You can be in the executive suite or the boiler room. Wherever you are, you are in a position of influence through your attitudes, your words, and your actions.

God wants us to have the boldness to use our influence to

share our faith. That means cultivating a confidence in God that He will do what He has said He will do. That means relying on the authority of God's Word and tapping into the power of the Holy Spirit. That means pushing past hesitation to take the gospel message to the people in your world. No matter where you are, God intends for you to be a living demonstration of confidence in Him and to have the courage to tell what He has done.

I once talked to a young man who was in the habit of carrying a small New Testament in his pocket and reading it whenever he had a few minutes. He had taken a job in a huge distribution center, and he began pulling out the little Bible and reading it during his break time. The break room was usually filled with people, and soon he and God's Word were attracting people who wanted to talk. Some were just curious about why he kept a Bible in his pocket. Others had questions or wanted to talk about the challenges they were going through. Every time he pulled out that little Bible, he had an opportunity to talk about Jesus. God said this about His Word: "It will not return to me empty, but will accomplish what I desire and achieve the purpose for which I sent it" (Isaiah 55:11). Never underestimate the power of God's Word to draw people in and give them the answers they need!

Maybe you're the only person in your office who loves Jesus. That's not a bad thing—that's a kingdom assignment! Keep a Bible in view on your desk and wait for people to ask you about it. Mention Jesus when the slightest opportunity arises. When your Jesus-story spreads and you begin to have openings to talk about what He means to you, you'll see that God has placed you there for a purpose. If you want to work where there are lots of Christians, you'd better get busy!

Do you live on a block where you and your family are the

only Christians? That's why God moved you there! He's given you a mission field on your own street. Read your Bible in your front yard and talk about Jesus at the mailbox. Become known as that person who will pray at the drop of a hat. When your neighbors are born again and serving the Lord, then you can move!

> One person with a God-perspective can make a difference.

One person with a God-perspective can make a difference—just one!—so don't ever lose sight of your importance to God's purposes. He has saved you and delivered you. He has given you leadership skills that are ready to be used. He has put you where you are for a season and for a reason. He wants you to speak up and make a difference for Him where you are. He wants you to let your love for Him shine so that people will want to know what He has done in your life.

BE READY TO STAND

What comes to your mind when you think of standing? Waiting? Boredom? Wasted time? I think we've imagined that standing is a passive activity that doesn't require much effort, but that's not true when we're talking about standing for the Lord.

I won't insult your intelligence by saying that standing for Jesus is always easy. It is not. It will require you to live with a purpose beyond what is on your daily schedule. It will mean putting Him before everything and everyone—even family, friends, and career.

It will require you to make daily decisions to stand both for godliness and against ungodliness. We are called not just to hold the ground we're standing on now but to look ahead for opportunities to take new ground. That means we are on offense and defense at the same time. We stand for truth and righteousness. We stand for holiness and purity. We stand against evil and against anything that threatens families or the church. We stand at home. We stand in the workplace. We stand in the community. We stand . . . and we keep standing.

This sounds like work, doesn't it? That's because it is! Whether in your home or your workplace or the public square, standing for God requires intentionality and determination. It means being prepared to go into spiritual battle against the dark forces that conspire against us. That is why God has provided us with spiritual armor that shields us from the evil the enemy throws our way.

BE PROTECTED

You've probably seen soldiers outfitted with an impressive array of body armor and protective equipment. I can't imagine walking around with as much as one hundred pounds of gear, but they wear it gladly because they know it will help protect them from attack and give them ways to defend themselves.

God has provided us with an even more impressive set of spiritual armor that is no burden to carry. He knows exactly what we will need in order to protect ourselves, and He has provided for every eventuality. Paul described this armor in his letters, in this passage to the Ephesian congregation: "Therefore put on the full armor of God," he wrote, "so that when the day of evil comes, you may be able to stand your ground, and after you have done everything, to stand" (Ephesians 6:13).

Note that Paul didn't say *if* the day of evil comes; he said *when* the day of evil comes. Paul wasn't talking about some day in the distant future when some hypothetical evil might touch us. He was talking about the evil that we will face every day and should be prepared for.

"Stand firm then," he continued, "with the belt of truth buckled around your waist, with the breastplate of righteousness in place, and with your feet fitted with the readiness that comes from the gospel of peace. In addition to all this, take up the shield of faith, with which you can extinguish all the flaming arrows of the evil one. Take the helmet of salvation and the sword of the Spirit, which is the word of God" (vv. 14–17).

Truth. Righteousness. Readiness. Faith. Salvation. The Word of God. This spiritual armor is available to anyone who will pick it up and wear it, but it is utterly useless to you if you leave it on the shelf of God's armory. It is God's desire that we go through life fully protected from the Enemy's arrows, so I urge you to take advantage of all the help He offers you.

BE READY TO PERSEVERE...

Do you know what it means to persevere? I don't mean the kind of perseverance that helps you finish a difficult crossword puzzle. I mean the kind of perseverance that keeps you standing when every message you're hearing is "Sit down!"

Serious runners understand this. Have you ever heard of "the lie of the first mile"? The idea is that during the first mile of a run, your body will send you a barrage of messages: "Your lungs are going to explode!" "You wore the wrong shoes!" "You'll never finish. Turn back!" This is especially true if you are alone. It is easy to think, "I can turn around and head for the house. No one but me will ever know." But experienced runners know that this is more than a physical battle. This is a battle of the mind and emotions, so they push through and keep going. They have learned what it means to overcome momentary discomfort and quiet the messages that tell them to stop. They have learned to persevere.

Following the Lord is about so much more than reciting a prayer and showing up for church a few times a year. People who think it is easy being a Christ follower are not Christ followers. They do not understand that it will require the very best you have—the best of your intellect, your character, and your strength of will. It will take all the determination you have, all the courage you can summon, and all the support you can find.

> **If you are to follow the example of Jesus and be His true disciple, you will have to endure opposition.**

Here's something you can count on: if you are to follow the example of Jesus and be His true disciple, you will have to endure opposition. You will have to persist when the conditions around you are not ideal.

AND PERSEVERE ALONE

The Bible gives many accounts of people who stood alone for God. They were filled with His power, but physically they stood alone and probably felt very exposed. Let's think about some of them.

Young David stood alone against Goliath while powerful Israelite warriors cowered in their tents. The power of God was with him, and he was victorious over the enemy. Later in his life he had been anointed king but was living as a refugee when his own men wanted to stone him. Once again, he relied on encouragement from the Lord and made it through a very difficult season.

Queen Esther left her handmaidens and advisors to approach the king alone, knowing that the penalty of displeasing him was certain death. God honored her bravery on behalf of her people, and they were saved from destruction.

Paul, the greatest of the New Testament evangelists, wrote of his companions abandoning him when he was in prison. He knew that the Lord was with him, but he still wrote to Timothy that he was cold and needed a coat. Even spiritual giants have physical needs.

The disciple John had been exiled on the island of Patmos because of his ministry for Jesus. In the midst of this solitary confinement, Jesus came to him and gave him a description of the end of the world as we know it and a vision of the future.

None of these situations were easy or pleasant, but these heroes of the faith stood . . . and kept standing. What about you? Are you willing to stand for Jesus in this generation? Will you be willing to stand for Jesus when your position is unpopular? When you feel misunderstood? When you don't have all the answers? When you're standing alone?

Will you be willing to stand and make your voice heard when your local school board is selecting textbooks and writing policies? When your city council wants to close churches but allow liquor stores to stay open? When your state government wants to provide funding to abortion clinics?

The problems we are facing today are not the result of the attitudes and behaviors of the ungodly people in our society. They are the direct result of the apathy of the people who say they believe in God. For so long we have been content to fill our churches with overlookers instead of overcomers. We overlook greed because we are striving for the same financial goals as the rest of the world. We overlook immorality because we don't want anyone to look at us too closely and comment about our own choices.

We overlook indifference because we are indifferent. We don't want to appear to be harsh or judgmental. Instead, we want to be seen as tolerant and inclusive. Don't get me wrong; I'm not asking you to be angry or agitated when you confront ungodliness in the world. I want you to be filled with grace and compassion. But I also want you to be filled with fear of the Lord and respect for His truth.

This I know: we can be either overlookers or overcomers. We cannot be both. When we are faithful to stand for Jesus, He will be faithful to stand with us. Yes, God may allow us to face opposition. But when we persevere, we will grow in our knowledge and experience of His faithfulness and display His power and love to the world.

The writer of Hebrews compared this life to a race. He

encouraged us to keep our eyes on our Savior and be ready to endure whatever comes: "Let us run with perseverance the race marked out for us, fixing our eyes on Jesus, the pioneer and perfecter of faith. For the joy set before him he endured the cross, scorning its shame, and sat down at the right hand of the throne of God. Consider him who endured such opposition from sinners, so that you will not grow weary and lose heart" (Hebrews 12:1–3).

Think about everything that Jesus endured to purchase your salvation. Remember the promises He has made to those who persevere. Do not grow weary. Do not lose heart, even in the face of opposition. Instead, follow in His steps with joy and anticipation of what He has promised to do.

SHORT LIFE. LONG LEGACY.

Our lives are short, but our legacies are long. Consider the legacy of Edward Kimball.

> In Boston, a Sunday School teacher named Edward Kimball led a shoe store clerk named D. L. Moody to accept Jesus as his Savior and Lord.
>
> D. L. Moody became a preacher and went to England, where his messages stirred the heart of a young pastor named F. B. Meyer.
>
> F. B. Meyer came to the United States, where his preaching was used to convert a student named Wilbur Chapman.
>
> Wilbur Chapman heard D. L. Moody preach, became his coworker, and employed an ex-baseball player named Billy Sunday as his assistant.

Billy Sunday became a great evangelist and preached at a
     crusade in Charlotte, North Carolina.
Billy Sunday's organization invited the evangelist Mordecai
     Ham to preach in Charlotte.
Mordecai Ham preached in the tent meeting where Billy
     Graham was saved.
Billy Graham proclaimed the gospel to millions in person
     and many more through his televised crusades.
Billy Graham's children and grandchildren continue his
     legacy of preaching and teaching today.[3]

Do you think that Edward Kimball had any idea of what his
spiritual legacy would be when he told that young shoe salesman
about Jesus? Of course not. But he was faithful to the invitation
that God had placed before him, and the rest is history.

HOW WILL YOU RESPOND?

In the early days of 2020, we began a journey that none of us
dreamed would last more than a few months. We were told to go
home for a couple of weeks until the worst of the coronavirus was
over, then we could get back to our daily routines. We've passed
one benchmark after another that we thought would put an end
to the unrest that was unleashed in that season. Instead of finding resolution, the confusion and division in our nation seem to
grow with each day, and COVID-19 is just one contentious issue
among many.

I believe that a spiritual revolution has begun, and its end
result is undecided. I also believe with all my heart that the

outcome will be determined by God's people. There are spiritual challenges confronting us on a daily basis, challenges that would have seemed unimaginable just a few years ago. They are challenges that will affect not only our lives but the generations who follow us. You may think that things won't be too bad during your lifetime, but what kind of world do you want your children and grandchildren to live in?

How will you respond to what is going on around you? Will you run and hide and hope that the Lord doesn't notice your absence? Will you stay in your seat and watch the action on the field, hoping that someone else will come along to fight for righteousness? Or will you put on the armor of God, then walk onto the field and take your place, ready to engage the battle alongside our Lord?

I am not naive. I know that it is not easy to see what is going on around us and filter it through a spiritual lens. I know that anger and despair are easier responses. I know that it requires focus and intent and determination to think in new ways and change attitudes and behaviors. I know that it requires tremendous courage and fortitude to stand up and push back against deception and evil.

Frankly, I think that many of us are simply having trouble looking forward. We are caught up in mourning a season that has passed, and much of our energy is focused on getting back there. I understand that sense of sadness and longing, but there is no going back. God did not leave the Red Sea parted in case the Israelites didn't like it on the other side. His invitation was for a one-way journey to something better. That is His invitation to us. That is the journey He is leading us on. So we need to be aware of what is going on around us and prepare ourselves for what is ahead.

The Bible tells us that one day Jesus will step back into history and make all things new. No event in Scripture has more prophecy directed toward it than His return to the earth. But He says that people will be self-involved and unaware on the day He is revealed. Most people will not be expecting Him, and they will be unprepared.

My heart breaks when I see people completely ignore or turn away from the gospel's message of salvation through the shed blood of Christ. But I also am concerned for the church, for you and me, that we have been lulled into a sense of complacency about our relationship with the Lord. It is easy to take God's mercy and grace for granted and live with half-hearted loyalty toward Him. It is easy to look like a Jesus follower when we need to for appearances' sake but live with a different set of standards when we are away from the church building and our Christian friends.

WHAT WILL YOUR SPIRITUAL LEGACY BE?

Make no mistake: The Lord's purposes will be accomplished, with you or without you. We know that Jesus' return on that fateful day will be triumphant. And we know that those who served alongside Him faithfully will be rewarded for what they have done.

With that in mind, what will your spiritual legacy be? Where will your loyalty lie? What will be your priorities for your brief days on the earth? Do you want to meet Jesus knowing that you did just enough to get by? Or do you want to meet Him knowing that you gave Him all you had, that you did everything you could to grow closer to Him, to bring more people into His kingdom, and to strengthen His church?

I do not want Him to see me on that day and say, "Oh. It's you." I want Him to greet me with a smile and say, "Welcome! And well done!"

You and you alone will determine how the Lord greets you on that day. You will not be accompanied by your parents or your spouse. Your small group leader will not be there. Neither will your pastor. This will be a conversation between you and the Lord, and all will be brought into the light—even the deepest desires and motives of your heart.

This conversation will be based on more than your recitation of the sinner's prayer. It will be based on the decisions that you make today, tomorrow, and every day until the Lord returns. Daily choices have eternal consequences; this is the message of Scripture.

My prayer is that you will live as if you will meet Jesus tomorrow. I hope you will feel that kind of urgency about your relationship with Him. I hope you will give Him your very best and hold nothing back. I hope you will begin to invite God into your calendar and daily schedule. And when you feel Him inviting you to join Him in His kingdom purposes, I hope you will say yes and pursue them with everything you have.

You know how the story ends. You know what it will mean to be on "the right side of history." I hope that you will determine in your heart to stand with the Lord and be counted among the faithful on that day. I hope that you will live in such a way that He will be able to say, "Welcome! And well done!"

PRAYER

Heavenly Father, You are the Creator of all things. You are Lord of the past, present, and future. You see the end from the beginning. I am humbled that You care about the details of our lives and have prepared a future for each one of us. I thank You that You have begun to awaken us to this most unique season. You are giving us perception, insight, and understanding. You are giving us ears that can hear and hearts that can receive in ways that seemed beyond us not long ago. Lord, we choose to turn our attention and our focus to You. You are our foundation and our strong tower. You are our deliverer and our hope. Through the blood of Jesus Christ, we have been delivered out of the hand of the Enemy. He has no power or authority over us, and we can rest completely in Your watchful care. Holy Spirit, continue to give us the awareness and discernment we need. Teach us to encourage and strengthen one another. Thank You for choosing us to stand for You in this time and place. We want to say yes to You with all of our heart, mind, soul, and body. May You be pleased with us and welcome us with joy on that great day. In Jesus' name, amen

NOTES

Chapter 1: Our Trust Eroded

1. Noel Langley, Florence Ryerson, and Edgar Allen Woolf, *The Wizard of Oz* screenplay, accessed March 9, 2022, https://sfy.ru/script/wizard_of_oz_1939.

2. "Mission, Role and Pledge," Centers for Disease Control and Prevention, accessed February 14, 2022, https://www.cdc.gov/about/organization/mission.htm.

3. Phillip Kane, "The Great Resignation Is Here, and It's Real," *Inc.*, August 26, 2021, https://www.inc.com/phillip-kane/the-great-resignation-is-here-its-real.html.

4. Jason Plautz, "The Environmental Burden of Generation Z," *Washington Post* magazine, February 3, 2020, https://www.washingtonpost.com/magazine/2020/02/03/eco-anxiety-is-overwhelming-kids-wheres-line-between-education-alarmism/.

5. "Critical Race Theory," Heritage Foundation, accessed March 9, 2022, https://www.heritage.org/crt. I highly recommend Voddie Baucham's excellent book, *Fault Lines*, which explores the origins of critical race theory and its implications for the contemporary evangelical church. Voddie T. Baucham Jr., *Fault Lines* (Washington, DC: Salem Books, 2021).

6. "New York City Police Officers Have a Question . . . What Did You Think Would Happen?" New York City Police Benevolent

Association, accessed March 9, 2022, https://www.nycpba.org
/media/36654/200710-news.pdf.

7. Sara Cline, "As Violence Surges, Some Question Portland Axing
Police Unit," AP News, March 6, 2021, https://apnews.com
/article/race-and-ethnicity-shootings-police-violence
-coronavirus-pandemic-704eeab551b452658cf2fa91a123b483.

8. Hemal Jhaveri, "Oral Roberts University Isn't the Feel Good
March Madness Story We Need," For the Win, March 23, 2021,
https://ftw.usatoday.com/2021/03/oral-roberts-ncaa-anti-lgbtq
-code-of-conduct.

9. Renita Coleman et al., "Why Be a Journalist? US Students'
Motivations and Role Conceptions in the New Age of
Journalism," ResearchGate, December 2016, https://www
.researchgate.net/publication/312357298_Why_be_a_journalist
_US_students'_motivations_and_role_conceptions_in_the
_new_age_of_journalism.

10. Brent Barnhart, "41 of the Most Important Social Media
Marketing Strategies for 2022," Sprout Social, February 3, 2021,
https://sproutsocial.com/insights/social-media-statistics.

Chapter 2: The Church Shaken and Church Exposed

1. "Methodology," Pew Research Center, Religion and Public Life,
July 15, 2019, https://www.pewforum.org/2019/07/15
/methodology-26/.

2. "Christian Persecution," Open Doors USA, accessed February 14,
2022, https://www.opendoorsusa.org/christian-persecution.

3. *Calvary Chapel Dayton Valley v. Steve Sisolak*, Global Freedom
of Expression, Columbia University, accessed February 14, 2022,
https://globalfreedomofexpression.columbia.edu/cases/calvary
-chapel-dayton-valley-v-steve-sisolak/.

4. Supreme Court of the United States, *Calvary Chapel Dayton
Valley v. Steve Sisolak, Governor of Nevada et al.*, July 24, 2020,
https://www.supremecourt.gov/opinions/19pdf/19a1070_08l1.pdf.

5. Dietrich Bonhoeffer, *The Cost of Discipleship* (New York: Touchstone, 1995), 43.
6. "Living the Commitments: The Vanderbilt Divinity School's Ethical Statements," Vanderbilt Divinity School, accessed March 9, 2022, https://divinity.vanderbilt.edu/about/Living%20the%20Commitments.pdf.
7. "Americans Oppose Religious Exemptions from Coronavirus-Related Restrictions," Pew Research Center, Religion and Public Life, August 7, 2020, https://www.pewresearch.org/religion/2020/08/07/americans-oppose-religious-exemptions-from-coronavirus-related-restrictions/.
8. "The Weapons of Our Warfare—Divine Power at Our Disposal," World Outreach Church, August 1, 2020, https://www.youtube.com/watch?v=8TvZZGZ9dT0.

Chapter 4: Fundamentals Matter

1. Robbie Gonzalez, "Free Throws Should Be Easy. Why Do Basketball Players Miss?" Wired, March 28, 2019, https://www.wired.com/story/almost-impossible-free-throws.
2. "Bob Fisher," Guinness World Records, accessed February 14, 2022, https://www.guinnessworldrecords.com/search?term=bob-fisher.
3. Jon Miltimore, "Why Chick-fil-A Is So Much More Efficient (and Friendlier) than Government," Foundation for Economic Education, February 2, 2021, https://fee.org/articles/why-chick-fil-a-is-so-much-more-efficient-and-friendlier-than-government/.
4. "Concrete Testing," Concrete Network, accessed February 14, 2022, https://www.concretenetwork.com/concrete-testing/.
5. David Maraniss, *When Pride Still Mattered: A Life of Vince Lombardi* (New York: Simon & Schuster, 1999), 274.
6. "The Bible Reading Plan," Allen Jackson Ministries, accessed March 9, 2022, https://www.thebiblereadingplan.com.

Chapter 5: Inside Information (A Biblical Worldview Gives Insight)

1. *Merriam-Webster*, s.v. "worldview," accessed February 14, 2022, https://www.merriam-webster.com/dictionary/worldview.
2. "A Biblical Worldview Has a Radical Effect on a Person's Life," Barna Group, December 3, 2003, https://www.barna.com /research/a-biblical-worldview-has-a-radical-effect-on-a -persons-life/.
3. "Belief in Absolute Standards for Right and Wrong," Religious Landscape Study, Pew Research Center, 2014, https://www .pewforum.org/religious-landscape-study/belief-in-absolute -standards-for-right-and-wrong/.
4. G. Allen Jackson, *The Whiteboard Bible*, vols. 1–3 (Murfreesboro, TN: Intend Publishing, 2014–2015).
5. *Sydell STONE et al. v. James B. GRAHAM, Superintendent of Public Instruction of Kentucky*, Legal Information Institute, Cornell Law School, accessed March 9, 2022, https://www.law .cornell.edu/supremecourt/text/449/39.

Chapter 7: The Path of the Storm

1. "Monthly Weather Forecast and Climate Tennessee, USA," Weather.com, accessed February 15, 2022, https://www .weather-us.com/en/tennessee-usa-climate#climate_text_4.
2. Lee Edwards, "Three Nations That Tried Socialism and Rejected It," Heritage Foundation, October 16, 2019, https://www.heritage .org/progressivism/commentary/three-nations-tried-socialism -and-rejected-it.
3. James Bovard, "Don't Celebrate Karl Marx. His Communism Has a Death Count in the Millions," *USA Today*, May 5, 2018, https://www.usatoday.com/story/opinion/2018/05/05 /karl-marx-communism-death-column/578000002/.
4. "Most Americans Are Critical of Government's Handling of Situation at U.S.-Mexico Border," Pew Research Center, May 3, 2021, https://www.pewresearch.org/politics/2021/05/03

/most-americans-are-critical-of-governments-handling-of
-situation-at-u-s-mexico-border/.
5. "Did 2020 Shift Americans' Perceptions of U.S. History?" Barna
Group, June 30, 2021, https://www.barna.com/research
/perceptions-of-america/.
6. Jessica M. Vaughan and Bryan Griffith, "Map: Sanctuary Cities,
Counties, and States," Center for Immigration Studies, updated
March 22, 2021, https://cis.org/Map-Sanctuary-Cities-Counties
-and-States.

Chapter 8: Getting Ready

1. "PA Announcements Study Guide," AirlineCareer.com, accessed
March 9, 2022, https://airlinecareer.com/tests/pa-announcements
-study-guide/.
2. Corrie ten Boom with Jamie Buckingham, *Tramp for the Lord*
(Fort Washington, PA: CLC Publications, 1974), 55–57.
3. "Slow and Steady Wins the Race," Know Your Phrase, accessed
February 16, 2022, https://knowyourphrase.com/slow-and
-steady-wins-the-race.
4. James C. Collins, *Good to Great: Why Some Companies Make the
Leap . . . and Others Don't* (New York: HarperCollins, 2001).
5. I Walked Across America, accessed April 20, 2022, https://
iwalkedacrossamerica.com/the-list/.

Chapter 9: We Are Stronger Together

1. "Salt History: Salt Through the Ages," Morton Salt, accessed
February 16, 2022, https://www.mortonsalt.com/salt-history/.
2. Andrew Silver, "How Far Away Can You See Light from a
Candle?" Physics World, August 7, 2015, https://physicsworld
.com/a/how-far-away-can-you-see-light-from-a-candle/.
3. "Hospitality Is the Heart of Christian Households," *Households
of Faith* (Ventura, CA: Barna Group, 2019), 28.

Chapter 11: Eyes on the Prize

1. *Encyclopaedia Britannica*, s.v. "pantheon," accessed February 16, 2022, https://www.britannica.com/topic/Pantheon-building-Rome-Italy.
2. "Dietrich Bonhoeffer," The Dietrich Bonhoeffer Institute, accessed March 9, 2022, https://tdbi.org/dietrich-bonhoeffer/.
3. Dietrich Bonhoeffer, *Letters and Papers from Prison* (New York: Touchstone, 1997).
4. "Martin Niemöller: 'First They Came for the Socialists . . . ,'" United States Holocaust Memorial Museum, March 20, 2012, https://encyclopedia.ushmm.org/content/en/article/martin-niemoeller-first-they-came-for-the-socialists.

Chapter 12: Stand and Be Counted

1. John Maxwell, "Are You Really Leading, or Are You Just Taking a Walk?" August 7, 2012, https://www.johnmaxwell.com/blog/are-you-really-leading-or-are-you-just-taking-a-walk/.
2. Dick B., *New Light on Alcoholism: God, Sam Shoemaker, and A.A.* (Kihei, Maui, Hawaii: Paradise Research Publications, 1994), 453.
3. "It All Started with a Sunday School Teacher," Billy Graham Evangelistic Association, accessed March 9, 2022, https://s3.amazonaws.com/bgcdn/billygraham/dev/wp-content/uploads/legacy/pdfs/stepstopeace/Testimony_Article.pdf.

ABOUT THE AUTHOR

Pastor Allen Jackson and his wife, Kathy, live near Nashville, Tennessee, where he has served as senior pastor at World Outreach Church since 1989. Under his leadership, the church has grown from fewer than thirty people to more than fifteen thousand. His mission is to help people become more fully devoted followers of Jesus Christ, and his biblical messages now reach and encourage countless people through Allen Jackson Ministries.